Suffering
and *Joy*

The Meaning of Relationship

Richard Palanza

Order this book online at www.trafford.com
or email orders@trafford.com

Most Trafford titles are also available at major online book retailers.

Printed in the United States of America.

ISBN: 978-1-4669-1442-1 (sc)
ISBN: 978-1-4669-1441-4 (e)

Trafford rev. 02/03/2012

 www.trafford.com

North America & International
toll-free: 1 888 232 4444 (USA & Canada)
phone: 250 383 6864 ✦ fax: 812 355 4082

Contents

For my wife Dori, my daughters Jeanne and Dee and my grandson Luke.

I love you all very much.

This book would never have come to completion without the dedication and persistence of my best friend, Anthony Tiatorio. Although I had collected my thoughts and observations for an entire lifetime, Tony was responsible for encouraging me to share it all with others and for this I will remain forever grateful. Nor would it have been possible had it not been for my relationship with my beloved grandson, Luke and the inspiration he gave me to atone for all my past failures.

Preface

For some time now, I have wanted to write a book on the importance of relationships in my journey through life. This need has always been in me and I have now chosen to fulfill it. I know this because years earlier, through a dream, my unconscious told me so.

In my dream I am on a mountaintop in a range overlooking a rich verdant valley. The trees are sparse yet the peak is covered with wild green grass. The rugged mountains encircle a large crystal clear lake, flickering sunshine randomly glancing off its surface.

Simultaneously, I am in a college auditorium, standing on stage in front of the podium looking out into a room filled with students and faculty. I am not at all sure what I am to say or do. What is very clear is the realization that I have a small book in my back pocket, my wallet pocket, the pocket where my wealth resides, the pocket I am always aware of. Standing beside me is my high school class valedictorian.

Years later I now see the dream more clearly. This time I stand risen to great heights, like an eagle my vision is clear and is like the crystal lake. Moreover, I see an audience waiting to hear what I have to say. I begin to think of it as a duty to fill the empty pages of my book and I know that with my class valedictorian at my side, I will have the courage to try.

Introduction

Change Yourself Rather than the World

The key to life is happiness. Yet, happiness is a result and not an end in itself. For to be happy implies that you must be happy about something. That something is fulfillment. And, fulfillment implies a purpose for the something that makes one happy. Without purpose happiness is not possible and without happiness life remains unfulfilled.

Initially, our world is limited to ourselves and our mother whom we come to know and depend upon totally. In time, as our world expands we come to know and appreciate our father and being ourselves part of a family. Mother takes care of us with all her love, but there are times when she may not be able to fulfill our needs. Inherent in the good then is the possibility of the bad. And that bad inevitably occurs as a result of human shortcomings. The same may be said of our relationships with our father, the family and later with the neighborhood we grow up in, the school we attend and the nation to which we pledge our allegiance. Each level brings with it the capacity for both good and bad.

But if we accept our limitation that we are but a part of the whole, we stand a better chance of opening the heart, the source of compassion and forgiveness, the pathway to understanding and the manifestation of love and we become the good and a means to a higher end. If we do not accept our limitation and see ourselves as the whole itself, the head will lead, the source of egoism and vengeance, the pathway to misunderstanding, the illusion of will and the manifestation of passion and desire, we become an end unto ourselves and are dead.

Everything changes. No one remains the same. Everyone is on a path, either upward or downward. One's path is always contingent upon the various relationships each of us has at any one particular moment in time. Relationships never end but they always change.

How we view the ways in which others perceive us dramatically influences how our personalities develop. In essence, relationship is all. All parts relate to the whole and the whole incorporates all of its parts. Relationships are the most important aspects of our lives. In fact, they constitute who we are. Understanding their true nature is essential to the development and evolution of personal enlightenment.

Personal human relationships exist on many levels: parent, sibling grandparent, friend, colleague and neighbor. Yet often we restrict our thinking to the ways in which we relate to only the most intimate of our life's partners. Few consider fully the impact that this myriad of life's relationships has had. Consider for instance how one relates to a seashore or some mountains, perhaps a desert, a brook or stream, a field of wheat, a nest of flowers, or a nest of ants or even a nest of wasps. Moreover, one might consider their relationship with rain, sleet and snow as opposed to the warm sunshine and bright blue sky of a summer day and what it all means with regard to our attitudes.

Relationships impact our view of life as a series of opportunities or misfortunes. We should understand this force in our lives because it speaks to whether we develop an optimistic or pessimistic outlook, whether we feel rejected and abandoned or accepted and loved, worthy or unworthy, deserving or undeserving.

When I was a child my father told a very short story about me and repeated it periodically up to the time of his death. He called me "Cece" because I was small.

"Cece," he would say, "When you first began to speak you would point your index finger upward and with a big smile you would proudly say, 'I can hold up the sky with one finger.'"

I suspect his telling me and everyone in the family that story repeatedly, always in a warm, happy and laughing way, reinforced my feelings of pride, knowing that I was loved, that I was safe and worthy, and most of all that I was very capable, wonderful attitudes with which to embark on a life's journey. Why then I ask myself, am I not a great military general, a world explorer, or President of the United States of America? Those were my childhood goals, my dreams, and aspirations!

Yet, in a strange way, my childhood dreams did come true. I became the master or general if you will, of the many aspects of my own person. I have explored the history and psychology of both the physical and psychological world and their impact and have, as a person, evolved to preside over the realm of my world.

Chapter One
The Beginning

I suspect that the story of my life is very similar to yours or anyone's insofar as each of us is dealt a hand in life that restricts and limits, even imprisons us yet at the same time may well serve to potentially free and liberate us to become true individuals. One of those gifts to me was the set of traits I learned from my father.

I was the third eldest in a family of fifteen children. My father, a mason by trade, came to the United States from Italy passing through Ellis Island early in the last century. He lived with friends in New York City. Through those friends, he met my mother who was born and raised in Mansfield, Massachusetts. They were married and settled in New York where he applied his trade, working as a mason on the construction of the Empire State building.

I was born November 7, 1929, a few weeks after the stock market crash and the onset of the Great Depression. Growing up in a large family during the 1930's presented more than a challenge for my family. Work became scarce; times got hard. It was a constant struggle for my parents to provide adequate food, shelter, clothing, and medical care for our rapidly growing family. While there were many happy times, for the most part we suffered a relentless shortage of the basic necessities of life. Nevertheless I worked hard to cultivate an optimistic attitude in the face of poverty.

On one occasion when we were out of food and very hungry my father told a tale of when he was a cook in the Italian army in North Africa during the First World War. He and his comrades were captured by the Germans and held as prisoners. There was little to eat. Each soldier was allotted two slices of bread but there was, he continued to say only one slice of salami. He told us how he tied a long string to it and attached it to the ceiling. He then told the hungry men, one after the other, to clap the meat with their bread and to enjoy their salami scented sandwich. I know now that he told this story to make us laugh, to help us forget our hunger, and to raise our moods above a depressed state.

H aving to learn to share in order to survive, and that is just what we did at times, survive, inculcated strong tendencies and values of communalism, something akin to many tribal societies where individualism is suppressed. These effects adversely impacted my understanding of who I was and what was mine. In short, not understanding myself made learning how to be responsible to myself difficult. While I had acquired a strong set of values such as a sense of hard work, sharing with others, and an outlook of optimism, I had repressed, along with other early childhood traumas, much anger, fear and resentment. And, all of those repressed feelings triggered and manifested themselves through unconscious associations as misplaced anger toward people I truly thought I disliked. While I got along well in my relationships with some family members and friends, all those repressed negative feelings, my shadow if you will, plagued me throughout the first half of my life.

I t was early spring 1934. I was five years old playing in the backyard of our rented family bungalow in East Foxboro, Massachusetts. As would most young boys my age I delighted in finding and throwing small stones. The last stone I selected was a thin small piece of slate which I scaled sidearm, as any boy would, while standing in front of a pond, lake, or the seashore, hoping to see it skip several times in and out of the water before sinking to the bottom.

Suddenly I heard my father yell loudly, "Jesu Christi, que cosa?"

I became frightened and shocked to see the bewildered look on his face and the blood on his forehead and hand as he reached up to find and soothe his hurt. Then suddenly, I saw my mother, apron tied around her stocky mid-section, rushing outside to find out what the commotion was all about, the kitchen screen door slapping loudly behind her. I stood heart in mouth watching, unable to move, feet frozen to the ground shocked in time and space. I thought I had killed him.

It wasn't my idea but I went along anyway with my older brother Albert and his friend Johnny. "Here, carry these," Albert said. Unwittingly, I took the handle of an empty gallon paint can, three-fourths filled with roofing nails, and followed Albert and Johnny. We headed down Oak Street to Mechanic Street, then ambled along Sand Street before settling on a suitable place to undertake our mission. We hid in the tall grass that grew in the sloping gully along the road. When certain that no cars were in sight, we climbed up onto the pavement and put two rows of galvanized roofing nails across the entire width of the street.

Following a moment of gleeful review of our handiwork, Albert spotted an old sedan moving slowly toward us. We quickly jumped down into the gully and hid. As the car passed over the double row of nails I heard four distinct loud, clear bangs. The car stopped. When I finally dared to look up I saw an old man and his wife, startled out of their wits, standing in the middle of the road.

"Run," Albert shouted and in what seemed no time at all we were dashing behind someone's barn heading home.

I didn't think much about that incident for the rest of the afternoon, until a policeman knocked on our door looking for my father. I sensed trouble. They talked for what seemed like an eternity. Then my father came over to me, took me up into his arms and asked, "Cecci, did you put nails on the street?"

I couldn't tell the truth so I lied by shaking my head from side to side. My father, smiled knowingly, shrugged his shoulders, turned to the policeman and uttered, "Eh."

The policeman smiled, turned and left. I felt safe in my father's arms but I remained shaken for quite some time fully aware that I had done something terribly wrong. I had lied to the policeman and to my father.

"C'mon Rich, come out back with me," Uncle Skeets said carrying a .22 rifle as he took my left hand. He led me to the front of the garage looked up and pointed into the first of the three pear trees that grew along the driveway.

"See?"

I looked up, unaware of what he wanted me to see.

"See? See?" he repeated, "See the bird up there?"

Patiently, standing behind and leaning over me, he put one hand on my shoulder and pointed up to the sparrow still perched comfortably between two small branches. Unable to speak, I nodded, somehow knowing what was about to happen. He removed the rifle from his shoulder, placed my left leg forward slightly while guiding the gun down in front of me. He pressed the butt against my shoulder as he held the barrel aloft.

"Now aim," he directed. At the same time, from behind me, he squinted up the rifle barrel while guiding the finger of my left hand to the trigger.

"See? See? He's still there."

I tried hard to stop his finger pressing down on mine, but I couldn't. I stood in shock as the gun discharged and the tiny sparrow plummeted and fell with what in my child's mind was a deafening splat. I tried desperately to rein back the tears, but my eyes flooded, feeling not only guilt but also anger at having been deceived and used.

"Nice shot . . . nice shot," Uncle Skeets bellowed as he patted me on the back; while I only heard myself murmur over and over, "I didn't want to kill that sparrow."

It was hard for me to tell whether she was black with white spots or white with black spots. I found her one morning on a short chain attached to a metal stake driven into the ground, feeding on the green grass to the side of our bungalow. I named her Bessie.

I was cautious at first as I watched her mill and munch for what seemed forever. Her huge eyes bulging from the sides of her head seemed to reflect my image. I sensed that she knew I was watching yet it did not seem to bother her. By the end of the second day I braved stroking her nose with my fingertips and a few days later I played with her without fear. And, it wasn't very long before I began speaking with her, putting my arm around her neck while she, at times, was licking my fingers. Now and then, when she had mowed the grass down, my father moved the iron stake to a new area of fresh high grass.

My father had purchased Bessie as a newborn calf from his friend and neighbor Caesare DiMarzio. Caesare owned the bungalow we lived in along with the empty adjacent lot where my Bessie grazed and we played daily. He was a bald, stocky man with a powerful muscular upper body, jubilant in nature, always laughing aloud, and strutting with confidence. He lived on top of the rise behind us. His driveway rose uphill slightly for about a hundred and fifty yards. Our families were close in space and community, yet their house was huge while ours was tiny.

One day in Caesare's house, upstairs in a hallway that seemed to be endlessly long and foreboding, I had a strange experience. Ahead of me there appeared to be empty bedrooms, seemingly far away from the stairs and I became frightened as if lost and swallowed up by depths of an unknown. I feared Caesare. I sensed him to be like his house, warm and receptive from the outside but once inside, up into the depths within which he sleeps, I felt lost and frightened, as if being consumed by a strange perilous vastness.

One early Autumn day, late in the afternoon as I ran hurriedly into our yard, I hardly noticed my father busily cleaning the area around a block and tackle which held, hoisted on a chain, my beloved Bessie. Shortly, my mother summoned us to the dinner table that evening, which, like most Summer and Autumn evenings, consisted of three or four of my father's work planks on top of a couple of sawhorses covered with a tablecloth flanked by long benches to sit on.

Caesare, his wife Irene, and Amelia were invited to stay for the meal. As I innocently began eating the meat on my plate I heard Caesare and my father talking about how easy it was. It was not until that very moment that I realized! I choked hard. I stared intently at Caesare for a time and got the feeling my stomach would burst. I ran away as fast as I could. I don't remember where I went or for how long I cried. I do remember crying for a very long time.

My grandparent's house felt scary to me. They lived in a tight Italian neighborhood on a thickly settled short street they called Cat Alley. Entering the house from the front was nicer, with more windows and light but we always went around back. Deeper into the darker part of the house was the large kitchen with my grandparent's bedroom door directly off to the left and finally the dark foreboding back hall. The only light crept in through the small glass panes at the top of the back door. This was, to me, the scariest part of the house.

My grandfather spoke mostly Italian, with a loud voice which always sounded angry. Often he seemed to be yelling at Nona, blaming her for doing something wrong. On the other hand my grandmother was quiet, maybe too quiet. I did not understand her. When she smiled I didn't feel happy or safe because I was not sure whether or not the smile was real. I mostly felt that I could not trust anyone there, neither my grandparents nor my aunts who lived there with them, because I sensed that they looked down on us.

I remember some unpleasant things being said. "They have too many kids and can't take care of them."

That hurt. I felt cheap and poor; it was like they were ashamed of me and made me feel ashamed of myself. The worst of it all, I think, was that I believed it was true and I didn't want to be there because I didn't want to hear it. And, when it came time to sit at the table for dinner I did not want to eat, despite being hungry.

I guess it was fitting that my tonsils were removed in that house. It was a sunny day outside and the light pleasantly flooded the three front rooms giving no hint of the darkness ahead. The family doctor had what looked like a portable lamp stand with an aluminum globe-like lampshade attached to the top, but strangely without a light bulb. I got scared when I saw my sister's head disappear into it. "She's only going to sleep," we were assured, but not without a great deal of kicking and screaming we rightly noticed.

Then it was my turn. I was more frightened than ever before in my short life. My resistance played out internally. I trembled; it was like all my inner parts were playing a discordant symphony. Yet, before I knew it, I could no longer resist. I awoke in the upstairs bedroom with what felt like a terrible sore throat. I was hot and felt weak, unable to swallow and it hurt to talk. It was dark and creepy. I wanted desperately to go home, but my father said no to me, "You sleep here. Tomorrow you go home."

I slept fitfully, waking and falling off again periodically for some time before the dream happened. My body was attached to the bedroom ceiling and I was staring down toward the floor. I drifted involuntarily toward the darkness of the back hall. I could now see clearly, despite the blackness of the night, the landings at both the top and the bottom of the stairwell. I hovered along the ceiling facing downward into what seemed like a black abyss. Never before or since have I experienced such fright. I was helpless and hopeless, thinking I would be swallowed up into the blackness and killed.

For several years following that dream the nightmare recurred and I re-experienced the same horror over and over. It wasn't until I reached adulthood that I came to learn and understand the relationship between meditation and dreaming, but I was too young to understand the meaning and value of such experiences. To me it was just terrifying and not the kind of thing I would ever wish upon a child.

There is a relationship between early childhood trauma and the misplaced anger many of us suffer as adults. These traumas wounded the life of a five year-old boy by instilling fear which would permeate and be manifested in many, if not all, of my adult personality traits and characteristics. Guilt, resentment, and low esteem were a trio of branches rooted in fear that were to plague me for the rest of my life and is a curse from which few of us escape.

Little did I realize that years later my words as an adult would become more caustic than the bullet that killed the sparrow. I would suffer low esteem for assuming responsibility for such intolerably horrific behavior on my part in all of these episodes, all of which were rooted in fear. I would become an angry pacifist and as an adult, I would resist and contest authority while not owning up to my own misdeeds.

For many years, throughout my youth and early adulthood I paddled my boat upstream, fighting the current regarding my relationships, resisting authorities in all aspects of my life. My rebellious nature emerged unconsciously into a lifetime struggle to overcome the psychological and physical realities at play in my world. The acquisition of a belligerent, dictatorial, outspoken and at times caustic attitude was the means by which my true nature, my Self if you will, was silenced. Unbeknownst to me, I had become my own worst enemy.

I became rigid and egocentric. My thinking was polarized. I deemed others to be either good or bad and they naturally reciprocated in kind. The process reinforced and guaranteed its continuation. I was silenced by my own noise both inwardly and externally. I remained blind and asleep to my emotional dysfunction in a mechanical non-volitional way until I approached middle age. On the one hand, I felt unworthy. On the other hand, I had such exuberance for life that I saw myself as well placed and well received wherever I went.

It is important to realize that attitude is chiefly responsible for whatever successes or failures we meet with on our life's path. And, there is little doubt in my mind that the circumstances of our earliest childhood present us with the most significant, sometimes impossible, set of obstacles to ever fully overcome. Making a conscious effort to do so is a courageous struggle. Even a mere modicum of success will lead to enlightenment and knowledge of the real meaning of happiness. Happiness is the result of a conscious effort, combating all that was long ago repressed within the hidden chambers of each person's being. As C. G. Jung once said, "If you don't confront your shadow, it will consume you."

Chapter Two

Growing Up

The kick-the-bar game we were playing at the end of the long gravel driveway came to a sudden halt as we all turned to see who was driving the new shiny deep blue truck. It was Papa! He was wearing his happiest face, one reserved for the rarest of times, a face that told me he felt he had struck gold. It was later that I learned the sad significance that truck would have for my young life.

We took turns sitting up front with him for short rides until everyone had had a turn. It was the smoothest ride I had ever experienced, traveling down the gravel driveway onto Central Street for a mile or so and then back home again. I often wondered whether or not I was any less happy about having the new truck than he was, at least not until I discovered that our new truck would soon carry us all away. It was during the summer of 1939 that my father, a self-employed mason who had experienced a rather long period of intermittent employment, thought the prospect of finding work would be better in Hartford, Connecticut than it had been in Mansfield.

For me, and I suspect for my brothers and sisters as well, the hardest part was leaving home. Home was and still remains, who I am. At that time it was everything to which I was connected. Home was more than the land our house sat upon, our yard and beyond; home was Atwood's field where I ran and played with my siblings and friends and the stream running through it where I fished for the first time in my life. Home was Foolish Hill where we hiked on warm summer days and skied in the cold winters; it was the abandoned gravel pit we called the canyon where we played Cowboys and Indians and cooked hot dogs and toasted marshmallows over an open fire and peeled the scorched black skins from the baked potatoes we dug out from under the dying coals. Home was going to Nellie's for a Hoodsie or some penny candy or a Pepsi and a Devil Dog. Home was savoring those treats and owning the privilege of sitting in either of the two booths Nellie kept stocked with comics and Big Little Books.

But by far the hardest part of going away was saying goodbye to my friend Jimmy. And as I think back, the worst of that was that I didn't, or rather, I was not able, to overtly make any more of losing him than of anybody else or any other thing. I would be deeply bothered by that for the rest of my life. Not until much later was I able to demonstrate openly my feelings of loss.

I can still see Jimmy standing in the driveway the day we left. It was a warm sunny August morning. He stood outside looking into the truck. My mind told me as I peered into his eyes that it was to be just for a while. I will be back. Our house is still our home. Despite the laughter and hand waves and the good bye, so long, see you later, his eyes like mine were filled with tears as we backed away from the house and headed south.

I can't say much about my fifth grade school in Hartford. I do remember playing and climbing the jungle gym during recess. It was fun, but despite having earned a perfect report card, I can recall very little else, what we studied, talked about in class, and what projects, if any, we completed. Yet, I do remember liking school. I liked it because of my teacher.

She was tall and slender. She was always neatly dressed, wearing high heels with nylon stockings, face framed with black hair worn close to her head and tapered down to her neck. Red rouge and lipstick starkly offset her pale complexion, framing her face off against her solid jet-black hair. I thought she was very pretty.

She never raised her voice at any time during the entire school year. If she had reason to speak with an unruly pupil, she would approach, lean over and make suggestions, inaudible to everyone else. I liked her. I liked her because I felt safe and comfortable with her.

I remember having the same feelings about my second grade teacher at the Paine School in Mansfield, who was the gentlest teacher I ever had. She too made me feel safe and comfortable. I remember having to "get the ruler" once for whispering to someone nearby. She walked over to my desk, quietly signaled me to stand and hold out my hand, palm up. I looked up obediently, following instructions without fear, never taking my eyes from hers. She grasped the back of my hand and proceeded to tap my palm gently three times. When her eyes signaled that the punishment had ended, I sat down, grateful for her kindness. I never again whispered in her classroom. It was a lesson I have never forgotten. I don't know if my teacher in Hartford ever gave the ruler to anyone in her class but I suspect that if she had, it would have been in the same loving way.

I guess my memory of these two wonderful women was heightened by the contrast they made with my fourth grade teacher. She was loud and threatening, nice at times, but severe with punishment. She used a variety of sanctions each in accord with the perceived severity of the crime committed. Minor infractions earned a seat in the wastebasket. More serious breaches found you sitting in one of her open desk drawers. For particularly devilish behavior it was an interminable time underneath her desk while she sat behind it! I remember well when my friend Jimmy had to sit under her desk. Later he delighted in telling the rest of us his version of that experience, which I'm sure contrasted greatly with her idea of what it was.

But the worst punishment I ever witnessed her employ was the sealing of a talkative girl's lips with adhesive tape. She was a shy girl with a rather plain face. Watching her inner response to what had to have been a very traumatic experience I felt as if I had swallowed a rock. For the rest of our school years, including graduation from high school, her face appeared to carry the scar from that cruel punishment. I remember well those women who treated others firmly but with a gentle persuasion, but were never unkind or angry. I have always appreciated them for parenting me, for filling a void in a way that my own mother couldn't.

My mother, herself physically and verbally abused as a child, was angry and at times abusive to me and to my brothers and sisters. If we were not fast enough to get away, which I usually was, she more often than not would use whatever weapon was at hand to take a swat at us. It seemed to me to be comical in a scary way when she would take after us with a broom. Willie, Albert and I would sprint to our three-decker bunkbeds where Willie got the worst of it on the bottom, Albert always took a whack in the middle bunk, but I usually escaped by scrambling over the top and through a hole into the attic.

It took many years and a lot of introspection before I was able to appreciate what a mother really is or how I felt a mother should behave. I have since come to understand that one of the things that drew me to those two gentle teachers and caused me to fall deeply in love with my wife, Dori, was the genuine kindness they embodied.

My parents took me along one evening to visit their friend Marietta, who lived in a first floor apartment near the market area on Front Street, close to the river. Anticipating our arrival she stood in the open doorway ready to embrace each of us with arms wide open and a smile stretched across her face, a smile that pulled me in like steel filings drawn to a magnet.

As we entered, the living room felt to me to be as mysterious as Marietta. The light from the floor lamp in the corner of the dimly lit room mimicked the flickering flames from the fireplace, driving my attention inward, causing dark corners to fade into everywhere and nowhere. I felt mesmerized, warmed and lured to the core of my being.

Marietta was a most remarkable woman. Full of life, she wore her long black hair partially wrapped in a red bandanna. She had a sharp but elegant nose and fiery eyes that offered what appeared to be an open invitation to become absorbed into her being. She sang and clapped her hands as she danced in front of the fireplace on the multicolored Persian rug. Her body swayed rhythmically when she walked like the limbs of trees seductively caressed by a gentle breeze. And later as I watched her sipping coffee, sweetened with anisette, periodically munching chestnuts roasted and toasted on the open fire, I thought of how young she looked and acted.

She was the most exciting woman I had ever seen. She had the appearance of a gypsy that lived in the moment, not fearful of other people's opinions, the reasoning of a Sufi if you will, that epitomizes the liberated Italian woman. She was the archetype of the prostitute. Her eyes ingested all upon which they focused. Her lips whetted appetites beyond her imagination. Her mouth signaled a welcoming union. Her smile seized and froze in eternal time the momentary gaze of others.

She was a woman in touch with her primitive self. Those who openly reject this woman are in denial of their own primitive subdued and repressed feelings. She represents the kind of woman every man longs to find, but for fear of the taboo imposed by the social collective of polite society, rarely do.

A young boy in the power of that seductive half of woman's archetype remains drowned and bound in infantile regression, unable to comprehend the meaning of those conscious and unconscious elements of womanhood. Nevertheless, Marietta danced that night in my ten-year-old mind. It wasn't until I was well into the fourth decade of my life that I began to understand, in my relationship with Dori, how wonderful it is to be in love with a whole woman.

Willie was the first of us to earn money by shining shoes and I couldn't wait to get my shoeshine box. It gave me my first paying job. I loved that little box which measured approximately 10 inches in width by 1 foot in length and was about 6 inches high. It had a footrest attached on a comfortable slant back toward the customer who would lean leisurely against the building at the edge of the sidewalk during the shine. The box was hinged in front, enabling access to any materials or equipment I would need to complete the job. And, the detachable shoulder strap made it easy to carry from one location to another. There was a sense of freedom walking along with that box strapped over my shoulder looking for business; it was fun, like fishing, if they aren't biting, I'd just move to another spot.

I gave nearly all of my earnings to my parents, as did my brothers. This early work experience established and laid a foundation for an irreversible lifetime belief in the old fashion work ethic. I charged five cents for a shine, the price advertised boldly on the side of the box, but more often than not, I got a dime. It was enough to buy a ticket to the movies. One more shine and I would have enough to have a candy bar during the film. At a very early age I felt a sense of exhilaration and gained personal satisfaction and pride knowing that I was able to do a job well enough to receive pay from strangers. It gave me a feeling of pride and self-reliance.

After a while, I found myself walking to places that reminded me of home. I especially enjoyed walking through Bushnell Park. Perhaps it satisfied a repressed longing I had for the outdoor-life back in Mansfield. I absorbed the beauty of the green lawns, the neatly trimmed evergreens of all sizes and shapes along with the scattered deciduous trees that looked so lonely in the late fall when their leaves abandoned their boughs. I often stopped to watch the squirrels chase one another around and up to the treetops and back down to the grass only to scurry into some nearby shrubbery. They looked to me like they were having as much fun as I remembered we did playing kick-the-can back home.

I spent countless hours in the Wadsworth Athenaeum, close to the Ancient Burying Ground. The epitaphs on the headstones fascinated me. Reading them stirred my imagination. I was carried back in time; I imagined and conjured all sorts of roles, which I acted out in my head. At the Athenaeum I became absorbed with studying the flags, coins, old books, various rifles, pistols and the military uniforms draped over headless mannequins. Most of the smaller holdings, especially the old coins, were enclosed in raised glass cases. I delighted in looking at them over and over by myself often until closing time. The museum fascinated me and started me on a lifetime love of history. I remember it began by reading and re-reading Kenneth Roberts' historical novels about on the French and Indian War.

When school got out for the summer my parents told us that we going home. As it turned out our move to the city hadn't made much difference. My father was not able to find any more work there than he had in Mansfield. I was ecstatic. Going home was what I really wanted. I dreamed about seeing our house on Atwood Street and especially seeing my best friend Jimmy.

That winter after we returned from Hartford, I learned to ski on Foolish Hill just beyond Atwood's Field near our house. It was a big hay field that measured approximately eight acres with a small stream dividing it into two parts. A flat stone bridge, covered with rich loam and matted tall grass, made crossing possible for the horse and wagon in the hot summertime during haying season. My friends and I would walk and ski across the field and bridge to the foot of the hills. I didn't have my own skis. Most of the time I took turns with my friend Jimmy.

The hillside was studded with trees, large Oaks scattered amongst predominately slimmer Maple, Birch and Cherry along with a thick layer of scrub bush on both hillsides of the trail. Over a long period, long before my time, I imagined that Indians walking the ridge of those hills had beaten the path over them.

The second hill became our favorite place to ski. It was the highest of the hills. Most of the time we skied down the trail along the ridge, at least until the dares began. The side of the hill was much steeper, faster, and more dangerous compared to the ridge and the trees and exposed rocks were thick, making it extremely fast and scary. This was especially so because everyone's skis were fastened with single leather straps and were very unstable. Yet, although it was much more dangerous, it was equally more thrilling. I loved to ski.

I had just turned twelve and we were on Christmas recess from school. Jimmy's parents had bought him a new set of skis for Christmas. They were the best, constructed with latches to secure them to his new ski boots. Oh, how I envied him and yet I loved him for giving me his old skis. Jimmy always shared everything he had with me. Ever since we met in second grade he was and remains yet my best old friend. Gleefully, I took my new skis and the poles home and stood them up on end beside each other in the back hall entry where I could look at them every time I passed.

That evening, as was their custom, my parents took their usual ride in the truck with one or two of my younger sisters. I do not recall whose turn it was to go with my parents that night. My mother had assigned Willie the dishwashing duty before she left. Albert and I were to clean the rest of the house.

Suddenly my two older brothers, Willie and Albert, got into a pillow fight. Although it began playfully, it soon developed into a donnybrook. Each had a pillow; both repeatedly threw their pillow at the other, back and forth, tempo and temper rising with the velocity of the flying missiles. I lay up in my bunk bed very close to the ceiling and the hole where I could quickly climb up into the attic any time I felt the need of a retreat from the chaos below. I remember the crackling of shattering and falling glass. I looked over and saw the pillow that Willie had thrown and Albert had ducked and avoided stuck in place in the broken window of the inside door to the back hall. The house suddenly fell deathly silent. Everyone scurried to bed and tried to fall asleep.

The next morning I couldn't wait to look at my skis. My heart leapt into my mouth. There they were, poles and all, smashed into little pieces.

"Ma, What happened?"

"Your father was so mad when he saw the broken window that he broke the first thing he could get his hands on."

I cried in both grief and incomprehension as to how my father could ever do such a cruel thing to me.

"Don't look at me," was my mother's familiar response.

Chapter Three

Teenage Years

Ｏne of my earliest jobs, when I was twelve years
old, was delivering newspapers for a news store
located on Main Street in Mansfield. After school,
I would ride my bike from the old junior high on Villa Street
to the shed in back of the store where all of the paperboys
met. I would load my Attleboro Suns, along with a couple of
Providence Journals into my bicycle carrier basket in front of
the handlebars and head out. My route covered the north end
of the town, up North Main Street to Oakland Street and all
the short streets branching off of it.

One of my stops was a tall three story brown shingled
home atop what seemed like a small mountain surrounded
by a high stone wall. There were many steps leading up to a
concrete sidewalk which spiraled even higher yet to the several
wooden steps leading onto the porch and to the front door. It
was not until after I graduated from high school that I learned
the significance of the woman who lived in that house and
that she would inspire me to reach for the highest good in my
own life.

Later, as my high school English teacher she unwittingly
awakened my passion for learning. She would sit upon the
corner of her desk with her skirt hiked and her long slender
legs crossed, reading to us from an open book on her lap. My
deepest and fondest memories of Mansfield High School are
those I experienced in her class and with her as my teacher
and for that I feel nothing but gratitude. She introduced me to
the English poets: Robert Burns, *Ode to a Field Mouse,* Keats'
Ode to a Grecian Urn, Percy Bysshe Shelly's *Ozymandias,* and
Alfred Tennyson's *Crossing The Bar.*

I found myself yearning to know the truth about such
things as the nature of the universe, freedom, eternity, and
immortality. But most of all I wanted to know the truth about
my own life. My reverie was ever interrupted and haunted

by such questions, prompting a perpetual life-long inner disturbance, constantly seeking ultimate resolution. And so I read ravenously over a lifetime of formal and informal education. I studied history, philosophy, theology, literature, mysticism, sociology, and psychology. Yet, it's not clear to me whether there was something about and within this one outstanding English teacher that inspired me to pay attention to the works and the questions these poets posed, around which my life revolved and evolved, or whether the questions evoked and sustained over a lifetime search for answers were already within me. What I do know is I will never find the truth; I can only know my truth.

I pedaled from Oakland Street across the grounds of Lowney's chocolate factory to the railroad tracks where I had to carry my bike across in order to continue on up North Main Street all the way to the last customer across from the Hercules chemical company tanks. The railroad tracks not only divided Oakland from North Main Street, they also decisively separated the sweet smell of chocolate from the dangerous caustic odor of the fuming chemicals. It was impossible for me to hold my breath long enough, but I tried. I tried every time. And every time, I failed.

Maybe it was because I knew that heading back down North Main Street I would have to pass the house of the biggest bully I ever had to face. He seemed to be three times my size. His body was shaped like a barrel, from his ankles to the top of his neck. I always relied on my quickness and it was nearly impossible for him to catch me. But one day he did.

"Hi, Richy." He sounded friendlier than ever before.

"Hi."

I wanted to give him the paper rather than walking past him to bring it to the door. Thinking better of it I decided to do my job properly so I laid my bike sideways on the ground and brought the paper to his front porch door. Then, as I turned he grabbed hold of me. It felt like I was in the grasp of a hay baler, about to be rolled up and wrapped with wire.

He knocked me to the ground and sat on me! My breath left me faster than a party balloon on the fly. Wiggling and squirming I finally managed to slide out from under his enormous carcass. I got up, jumped on my bike and peddled off as fast as I could. For years after that I nurtured the belief that I had fought off the big bully and escaped. It wasn't until we became high-school juniors that I came to know him better and realized that the demon was actually in me. He never meant to harm me. He was simply looking for a friend the only way he knew how and was nothing more than a big overstuffed Teddy Bear.

When I was thirteen my father asked me if I wanted a job. He told me that our family dentist was looking for someone to tend his horse and clean his barn. It meant that I would have to get up very early in order to get back in time for school. It was difficult for me to say no to my father.

For the first few days everything went well. I would take the feed from the hundred pound burlap bag that sat on a low platform in the barn. Then I would shovel the horse manure into the wheelbarrow, push it outside behind the barn and dump it onto the steaming pile.

One morning I found that the feed sack was empty. Not wanting to bother the doctor so early in the morning I decided to lug up a sack of feed from the basement myself. It was more than I had bargained for. I tugged and tugged until I moved the massive load to the foot of the bulkhead stairs, sat for a moment, then mustering all the strength within me, I was able to hoist one corner of the bag onto the first step, just enough so that it did not roll back. I jumped down behind the bag, reached under and pushed up as hard as I could until I was able to shove the rest of the bottom of the sack cleanly onto the first step. I repeated this feat six more times until it was out and on the lawn and little by little I laboriously dragged it to the barn. And as my reward, from that day forward, I found it to be my duty to replenish the feed bag when needed!

Feeling overwhelmed, I did not know what to do. Reluctantly, I told my father I was not happy with the job; that it was difficult getting up so early. He smiled. I felt he sensed there was more to it than I had admitted. Nevertheless, he explained to the doctor why I couldn't work for him anymore. It felt literally as though a load had been lifted off my back and I was happy again.

During my early teens I worked for Carl Gross delivering milk before the start of the school day. Carl, everyone called him Carlie, was the son of German immigrant parents who owned a dairy farm in West Mansfield. They had a huge white two-story home with a lot of rooms but I never went beyond the kitchen. We got to know them because my father had installed ceramic tile in their huge milk-room. I liked going there with my parents because they always gave us some homemade cake or pie.

Carlie had a wooden leg. He was what most called "a wild one," probably because he was a nonconformist and this was accented by the fact that he had lost his leg in a motorcycle accident. When I first knew him he was about twenty-one years old. Carlie like his parents was full of laughter, always sporting a smile. It was fun being with him and the work, delivering milk from the back of his pick-up, door to door while he drove, became easy because of his presence. The thought later occurred to me that I was attracted to Carlie because he seemed to manifest the kind of individualism that I repressed. For example, he would jump out from the driver's seat, hobble across the street with the clanking quarts for that customer, while I worked the other side. He would shrug off my mistakes with a "So, big deal; they got an extra quart today on the house."

Ordinarily the job would take about an hour and a half. But sometimes it took two hours. It all depended on Carlie's girl friend. If her mood were right, then I waited in the truck until he returned wearing a satisfied smile over his sheepish grin. Finally, like clockwork, he drove into the center of Mansfield to the diner adjacent to the A&P market where we always had coffee and I would get a huge sugar frosted cinnamon roll and then he would give me a quarter to take to school. He never deviated from this ritual. In addition to my pay of five dollars a week, he always gave my mother whatever milk she felt we needed and he always gave me an extra quarter.

It struck me later how much I was like Carlie's big German Shepherd dog that I loved to watch running, side to side, herding the cows from the pasture into the barn. You could see that he always looked pleased when his job was over because he would run to his master, sit up for approval for a job well done, while basking in the warmth of the hand rubbing gently across the top of his head.

Once man is reduced to his component parts he no longer exists, unless somehow all the parts unite once more into a whole. Thinking is the foundation for society and its institutions but simultaneously it is the demise of personal freedom for all who are incapable of maintaining true relationships and remain detached. Yet, where does one go with detachment, letting go, letting be? Must we resort to finding and living solely among other detached people? If that be the case, is it at all possible to remain detached in a society of detached persons?

Over the years, each time I saw Carlie he was the same happy-go-lucky person wearing a smile and greeting me, arms wide open. Not long after that I learned from a friend that Carlie had passed away. He could not yet have been fifty years old. I've thought a lot about why I remember him so fondly. Even though I had older brothers, he was what I dreamed an older brother should be. He was kind and considerate and generous, but most of all I knew that he loved me.

In high school I was a big sports star. I was voted most athletic. In football, as quarterback I called every play. I captained the basketball team and on the track team I ran the mile and won every race but one. But it was that single loss that I remember best. During the first three-quarters I kept my pace even with his. Amid the roar of the fans with less than a quarter mile to go his grunts grew louder as he slowly inched ahead. I was determined not to begin my kick until I reached the two-twenty yard marker but by then his lead was too great. All I had left was not enough; I lost my last high school mile run by less than a yard. Much later, coming to terms with that loss I came to realize that nobody wins all the time and that the important thing was not the winning or the losing but in taking individual responsibility for making my own decisions.

We had received the ball on the opening kick-off near our own twenty yard line. We had punched out three consecutive first downs reaching about mid-field. It was fourth down and one yard to go for a first down and the coach sent Ralphie in to punt. In the huddle, I told Ralphie to fake the kick and take off around the right end. I felt the element of surprise and the fact that he was the fastest runner on the team meant the first down was ours to be had. Wrong! Ralph was caught from behind just short of the line of scrimmage. We turned the ball over at mid-field and several plays later they scored what would be the winning touchdown.

That day an All American football player then playing professionally for the Los Angeles Rams talked to us at half time. Aiming his words directly to me he said, "Rich, never run on fourth down when you are on midfield; always punt."

Later in the season the situation repeated itself and we found ourselves at mid field with fourth down and a yard to go following three successive first downs. Seeing that same famous face in the stands and recalling his expert advice, reluctantly I called for a punt. During the half he came into the clubhouse again, looked at me again and said, "Rich, you had the momentum with three first downs in a row, why punt with a yard to go?"

It was one of those times when sooner or later in every one's life one faces a situation where any answer could be inappropriate. I simply swallowed hard and looked down in wonderment. Once again I realized that win or lose I should always follow my own judgment.

The summer after we graduated I worked for Mansfield's Highway Department with my friends Jimmy, Bob, Tommy, and Eamsie. Tommy was older. He graduated a couple of years ahead of me and was studying to become a veterinarian at Kansas State. Eamsie was one year ahead of me and was home for the summer from a prep school some place along the Hudson River. Bob was heading for Mount Herman Prep for a year before entering Cornell and Jimmy was accepted into Brown. I had just graduated with the class of 1947 but had no plans for college. I envied all of my friends. I wanted to be going to college somewhere that coming September too.

The work for the Highway department varied with the day of the week and the weather. Some days were slated for rubbish pickup and the rest of the week we cut brush along the side of the rural roads of West and East Mansfield and hauled it to the town dump. The driver was an older man named Joe who stayed in the truck all day only getting out to stretch his legs on occasion. At first Joe was a mystery to me but one day I learned a little about him and more about myself.

Rainy day work was the worst. Despite the raincoats and rain hats it was impossible keep from getting soaked. It was a steady plodding all day and it was boring. Sometimes four of us were assigned to Joe and we would work in pairs on the relatively narrow back roads. We would tell jokes and make up unbelievable stories trying to make the time pass and the work more fun.

One day, parked on the side of the road during a ten minute break Joe overheard me, Jimmy, and Bob talking about making out with our girls. For some reason he suddenly said to Bob, "If I had ten minutes with your girl I would be able to get her to do anything I wanted."

Bob responded angrily, "Horse shit, she wouldn't have anything to do with you."

"All I'd have to do is find and touch her spot and she wouldn't let go of me. She would let me do whatever I want and that's no shit."

"Balls," Bob retorted. I could see he was angry. He loved his girl and later they were married.

"Oh yeah, there isn't a woman alive that would resist it. Your girl is no different. They're all the same. She wants it."

By then Bob was furious. For me, it was uncanny to watch old Joe behave and argue like a teenager, with a teenager! Joe's incredible ignorance shocked me. Thankfully, Bob walked away and Joe got back behind the wheel of the truck. The last two hours of the day dragged on pitifully. I felt afraid knowing that in a few short weeks all my friends would be leaving for a better life and I would be left behind.

During the last week of the summer, while standing in the town yard near the driveway from the barn I saw two men get out of a new black sedan and walk toward where Eamsie and I were standing.

"Hey there! How's it goin'?"

"OK," Eamsie replied. "Rich, this is Dutch, my coach last year."

We exchanged hellos and Dutch went on to tell Eamsie that he would be taking a new position as head coach at a prep school in Connecticut. He went on to say that he was on the road recruiting ballplayers and asked if Eamsie would be interested in changing schools and playing for him again."

"Sure," Eamsie said, the thought of transferring to a new school didn't seem to frighten him. Then he said something that totally surprised me.

"What about him?" he asked as he swung his arm in my direction. "He's a good quarterback."

I wasn't very big and the coach looked doubtful, "You're a quarterback?"

"Sure am."

"Why not? See you both in two weeks." He gave Eamsie and me a copy of instructions for what to bring and how to get to the school. It's strange how things happen that way. I thanked Eamsie for recommending me. Always soft-spoken, gentle and kind, polite and diplomatic, he understood and returned my gratitude with a wide smile of deep and enduring friendship. So it was that my summer ended on a note of joy.

I could hardly wait to get home to tell my parents that I would be going to prep school in a couple of weeks. I wondered what it was going to be like in a prep school. I wouldn't be around to work with my older brother Willie and Papa. I knew Willie would be angry but I couldn't pass this up. I was going; I was going to school after all. My heart was pounding with joy.

R omford Prep School was nestled in Connecticut's Litchfield Hills. Treetops towered on both sides of the road whispering and dancing to the tempo of the breeze, cooling, amusing and a bit frightening at first, but soon we emerged into the sunshine and turned onto the school grounds. Perhaps the most important gift I received through my tenure at Romford was the natural expanse the school campus offered. During my alone time I relished my relationship with the solitude and serenity during my frequent long exploratory walks amid the hills where I always found for myself the time to ponder and to be at peace with nature and myself. But that wasn't why I was there. I was anxious with the creeping realization that a new era of freedom and responsibility was about to begin. I was leaving home! From that moment on, I would be free to choose my own path. My psyche was more captive to my newly acquired freedom to make my own way in life than it was to my responsibilities.

The football team was scheduled to report for practice during the last week in August, a week before the school opening. Several players were milling around and I introduced myself. "Am I at the right place?"

"I'd say so," one of them, sporting a freshly cut Mohawk haircut said, pointing toward one of the dorms. "Just go over there and choose a room."

His name was Joe. He was from Jersey City. He asked if I would like to be his roommate. My immediate impression of Joe was that he was a warm, outgoing, no-nonsense person, in command of himself. I was glad I met him. Joe was at least six feet tall and approximately one hundred and eighty pounds of solid muscle. I suspect that even Charles Atlas himself might have envied him. He could throw a football with uncanny speed and accuracy up to seventy yards and punt as far as eighty in the air. His skills on the basketball court were as superb as were his football skills and the same was true with bowling or any other physical thing he wanted to do. The year after our stay at Romford, Joe became the freshmen national punting champion at Duke University.

Joe looked after me everywhere we went. It became a habit on Saturday night to go into town to see a movie, to bowl, and have a beer. One night a group of town toughs confronted me for no apparent reason other than maybe because I was the smallest. Instantly Joe bolted to my defense, grabbing the bully by the scruff of the neck and hoisting him up to eye level. He looked directly into the boy's startled eyes driving a sharp dent with his fist into the fender of a parked car. "Try anything foolish and that's what you and your friends will get." I felt a sense of awe at how decisively Joe had ended that confrontation, yet the damage he left to some innocent person's property has always bothered me.

Chapter Four

Another Beginning

The path leads to home within oneself. I am presented with the freedom of choice from life's offerings. If I awaken within, I will arrive at my destiny. I will have attained enlightenment, happiness, and real love by carefully listening and observing what other human beings and nature have to offer. If I remain asleep, accepting what comes without conscious scrutiny and deliberation, I will suffer my fate. For me, the journey of life is to walk my path in unison and harmony with all of life's guides.

I try to understand the people who enter my life, the why of my acquaintances, and the depth and lessons they have for me. Some relationships are short lived while others remain alive for decades. Seeking the common thread among them gave me greater insight into the meaning of my own life. I now better understand the connection between all of my relationships, both positive and negative, and how they drove me to my destiny.

We met at Sandy's Clam Bar on Belmont Street in Brockton. It was a Saturday night in mid-August, the summer of 1948. Jimmy and I decided earlier to meet the two Eddies and head down town to the North Common to hang out a bit. Then we bumped into Lalo. Lalo's name is Roger but everybody always called him Lalo; I have no idea why or what it means. But Lalo had secretly borrowed his father's old pick-up truck and that gave us wheels. We decided to meander over to Card's Field to have some fun at the carnival.

We could hear the music and the voices of the crowd along with an occasional barker hoping to lure people to his station. Laughter mingled with the variety of music and the sounds of the differing rides of the Ferris Wheel, Merry-go-round, chairs on chains and the flying airplanes drew us in.

It was getting close to eleven o'clock and the carnival was ending when I decided to try my hand at the Ring Toss game. As it happened, following nine failures, during my tenth attempt, the rope ring I tossed bounced off a dowel and rolled directly back to me. I quietly picked it up and was about to toss it once more, which I knew was wrong. Just then the old woman who ran the game, angry as a hornet, rushed up directly in front of me and demanded that I surrender the ring to her.

"Ha, Miss America of 1903," I wisecracked and my friends laughed.

The sting of my insult caused her husband to come running toward me. He thought I wanted to fight. I didn't. But he called the nearby police officer to his side. It was Walter, a local cop that I knew and respected. I felt relieved.

After Walter heard the man's side of the story he came over to me and asked me what happened and I told him. He pondered a moment. I could feel his empathy for me. He knew me well. He had watched me play football and basketball many times. After a moment he turned and spoke wisely to me, as would Solomon. "Richy, it's late. The carnival will be ending in an hour. Why don't you guys just call it a night and leave?"

"Fair enough," I said and thanked him.

We headed out of the fair grounds to where Lalo's father's truck was parked. For some unknown reason he drove east toward Brockton. Never before had we visited Brockton. It had always been Norton, Attleboro, North Attleboro, Foxboro, maybe Wrentham, or Franklin, but never Brockton. Yet, when Lalo pulled up and parked we found ourselves in front of Sandy's Clam Bar on Belmont Street. Jimmy and I jumped off the back of the pick-up while Lalo and the two Eddies slid out from the cab. It was about 11:30. We set out to explore and have something to eat at Sandy's.

I quickly caught a whiff of the air with the mixed smells of French fried potatoes, onion rings, and clams. Waitresses in white dresses were busy taking orders, serving small seated groups and clearing dishes from the tables where others already had eaten and left. It appeared busy and friendly with groups of people who seemed to know each other.

Then I saw her. She sat on the opposite side of a partitioned half-wall facing the restaurant door in a booth with two other girlfriends. I walked immediately to the booth adjacent to her, smiled and said, "Hello, my name is Richy."

It was as though we were sitting at the same table hampered only by a low wood paneled divider. She was wearing a fitted three-quarter length black jersey that had a rectangular neckline with small semi-circles, cut slightly above her full breasts, exposing most of her shoulders and accenting her long slender neck. Somehow her beautiful brown eyes spoke to me. The allurement of her full lips, her slightly turned up nose and her flowing golden brown hair, her warm and inviting smile made time stand still.

"Hi, I'm Dori," she coyly responded.

I then asked if she would give me one of her fried clams. She smiled while slowly pushing her plate forward an inch or two, then saying silently with her slightly raised arms, "Help your self."

I reached over the partition and carefully took one clam, dropping it into my mouth, playfully exaggerating its tastiness while never taking my eyes off of her. We talked. She and her girlfriends had arrived by bus from the Saturday night dance at the Canoe Club in West Bridgewater. They had already called a taxi to take them home.

Too soon the taxi came and I knew it was time for them to leave. But I didn't want to let her go. I had to work fast. One of the girls walked around the back door of the cab and sat next to the rear window. I opened the door on the passenger side and told one of the Eddies to get in. Holding the door open I invited Dori to sit with them in the back seat and then I slid in beside her before anyone realized what happened.

Four in the back was crowded and I made my move. I reached over and lifted Dori onto my lap. She didn't seem to mind; by then, everyone was laughing. As the taxi moved out, I became intoxicated with the warmth of her slim and shapely body pressing down and against mine, my arms around her waist, her hands in mine, and the smell her freshly shampooed hair and the way her upper body moved about while talking.

It was a very short ride to the house on Main Street in Easton. Everyone got out of the taxi. Jimmy, Lalo and the other Eddie had followed in the truck. I was unaware that Dori had planned to sleep over with her friend. So when I escorted her to the front door to say goodnight I thought we were at her home.

"Would you go out with me?" I dared.

"Yes." She replied softly.

She's going out with me, I heard myself gleefully repeating over and over all the way back to Mansfield. She's going out with me.

Now, over six decades later, holding her close from behind in my arms as she sleeps, I recall my thoughts of that first meeting and our early years together.

For the longest time, I had idolized her; I had placed her upon a pedestal and she became an easy target for my misplaced anger. And, it was not until I was able to resolve my early childhood traumas that I was he able to find my true place with her beside me. Yet, I remained puzzled as to how I had been able to please her the night when we first met. I reflected once again on the low partitioned wall which had separated us in the restaurant. Had that been a symbolic omen?

Tonight she lies sleeping. My hands glide softly over and around her as I reflect on how nature and time subtly wreaks havoc on her body. I gently caress her now bony arthritic fingers and still bask in the warmth of her familiar form. I recall that moment of destiny when our eyes met that night at Sandy's Clam Bar so long ago and discover that it was as if I had been directed by some force toward everything I said and did that night. Never had my heart and mind spoken to me so coherently in such unison. I was enthralled beyond joy. I was then, and remain now, a very happy man.

I was in boot camp when the telegram arrived. It had been a long hot day in the field. I sat on the barracks steps and read it over and over again with shock and horror approaching impending doom. My father had inoperable cancer of the pancreas.

I cried, softly at first, for a long time. Then a kind of reverie interrupted my tears. I began remembering my father and his relationship with me. And, I experienced once again, with him, that early summer morning when I was about seven years old and was gently awakened by a whisper. Looking up I saw him leaning over me, with his finger vertically across his lips.

Taking me by the hand he ushered me out the back door into the blinding warm early morning sun. I sat on his lap. His arms around me, he pointed toward a beautiful peacock ablaze with brilliant reds and majestic purples. The peacock posed proudly for us and I felt very special. I never forgot this intimate moment that showed a part of him usually kept well hidden.

I thought about how he loved to read Ripley's "Believe It or Not" to make us laugh, wonder, and marvel at the various daily feats of human accomplishment. I also recall how freely he would laugh reading jokes aloud from the newspaper. I remembered too his attempts to ease his asthma by taking me with him in his truck for long drives at night up to high country he would say, up through Foxboro where the air was better. I remembered making wine together with the rest of my brothers and sisters every September when he brought home bushels of red and white Zinfandel grapes in his pick-up truck.

I also remembered the one football game he ever attended. He had made it clear that he didn't mind me playing, but he couldn't watch because he did not want to see me get hurt. And, sure enough, during the first period of that one game I had to leave with a cracked rib. My father had to leave too because he was unable to see me in the pain.

I requested and was granted an emergency leave. I flew home. His body was yellow, and that was frightening to me. And, despite being heavily medicated for pain, he suffered unbearably. I felt sad, scared and angry. I wrestled with remaining with him as much as possible and with not having to continually witness his suffering and pain. My world, it seemed, had come to a halt! Inoperable, no hope, nothing left but utter despair. It was a new and awful feeling. For the first time in my young life my optimism was shattered. I thought I would always have the courage to face any problem, but not this.

He was laid out in the living room in front of the picture window. His head faced the staircase toward the second floor. It was as if he were able to see through his lifeless and permanently closed eyes and look up at the ornamental plastered cornice he had so skillfully made. I gazed intently at his corpse. It lay still and cold in his coffin. Internally, I whisper to myself, he was a good man. Where has he gone? Who can say? And again, like Sisyphus, my hope turned to the fruitless rock of despair. I placed my hand upon his, leaned over the gray casket and kissed his pale cheek. Feeling the cold stone like corpse of my father's cosmetically powdered cheek sent waves of fear throughout my body. Ever since then I smell death in the roses.

I watched the endless parade of family, relatives, and friend's plod from the kitchen through the hall into the parlor where he lay. Each starring briefly before going back to pick up a plate of food or out the back door with a glass of wine or a bottle of beer. They congregated in and around the house. Loud and louder the laughter grew with the stories and jokes. I was raging within. My mind went out of control. How could they be so rude, so crass and so disrespectful and all the while drinking his wine; the wine I made with him and my brothers and my sisters?

D ori and I had been engaged for about a year. Since that first Saturday night when I was too tired to drive home sleeping over on the living room couch had become a habit. Her father, his name was Pelham, seemed to be OK about it at the time, at least he didn't express any negative feelings toward me or about our future wedding plans.

That Sunday morning I awoke to the smell of bacon and eggs with leftover baked beans from the previous night's dinner. Pelham greeted me with a warm wide smile and a welcoming, "Mornin' Richy. I fixed ye breakfast." I felt at home and happy.

I looked down toward my plate, with two perfectly cooked eggs, once over lightly, sitting precisely between two strips of bacon and a bit of leftover baked beans, on the other side. I was immediately taken by the fact that the three different foods were perfectly positioned so that no one of the groupings was touching either of the other two. I smiled thinking of how different it was from the meals I grew up with, all cooked in the same pot leaving a pile of what ever it was on your plate. I learned later that Pelham was excessively compulsive and that this often caused me to misread him completely.

After dinner, when we were alone, Dori told me that her father had a habit of rolling up all his neckties tightly and placing them neatly spaced in his dresser drawer, exactly the same distance apart. In that way, she said, he thought he could tell if anyone had been poking around in his things. I thought it odd that he should worry about someone poking around in his dresser drawer but I suppressed it along with many more instances of oddness about his behavior.

Sunday dinner usually consisted of a roast of some sort along with a yellow and a green vegetable and always with mashed potatoes and gravy. Pelham would proudly declare that dinner was ready and always precisely between three minutes before and three minutes after Twelve o' clock Noon.

Pelham ate English style with the fork in his left hand and the knife in his right. I would watch him deftly cut the meat on his plate, push vegetables onto his fork and amazingly to me eat his entire meal without once letting go of his tools. It was more sophisticated and polite I thought, so different from the way I was used to shoveling my food. I wanted to eat in the same way Pelham did, like the English. I wanted to feel that we were becoming a family.

Then it happened. "No one is ever gonna take my Dori away from me," he muttered as we walked up the front steps one evening. He was sitting in his chair on the front porch. His harsh words pierced the pit of my stomach and echoed that fateful telegram from home and the words, inoperable cancer. Hearing Pelham's remark ring over and over again and again in my mind, "No one's gonna take my Dori away from me," sent the same chill through my body. The faint twitchy smile emanating from his gaunt and ashen face, his hollow eyes staring straight through me into space gave me once again that horrible feeling of impending doom. I felt helpless. My world was toppling just as it had before.

As he leaned forward in his chair and began to rise we heard behind us an eerie groan followed by a rapid series of dull thuds as he fell and rolled rapidly down the front steps, smashing his head into the paved sidewalk. We stood speechless. Blood oozed from his mouth. His eyes were white as though he were looking up through the top of his head. Dori screamed with fright. She feared he was dying. "Call the doctor," I bellowed.

He came immediately. "Is he dying?" Dori asked her voice shaking.

"Hell no", the doctor chuckled, "He's OK; he's too drunk to get hurt."

Dori, always quick to respond to reality, adjusted almost instantly. She appeared to be able to go about doing whatever was necessary at any moment. I on the other hand stayed shaken beyond words. Something more was happening inside me. I was unable to comprehend my feelings. In both instances, in hearing Pelham's harsh words and in reading the news of my father's impending death, I was sent into internal flight from fear, but fear of what? I was not at all sure.

Later as Pelham lay sleeping in his upstairs bedroom Dori and I sat together downstairs in the living room. I comforted her with words of assurance "He will be OK; he's just drunk". Yet that awful feeling remained in the pit of my stomach and I could not help but secretly wonder if I would be OK.

Over the next several days Pelham recovered fully and his behavior appeared normal. It was then that he told Dori he wanted to pay for our wedding. I couldn't help wondering if it were from guilt or love. Nevertheless it appeared, at least on the surface, that he had resolved the issue of losing his daughter and everything seemed normal until that fateful night several weeks later.

It was Sunday. We all decided to go out for clam rolls. While sitting in the restaurant and halfway through our meal I looked up at him. He was wearing that eerie grin again; it once more pierced my stomach. The trust that I thought had been restored seemed once again to be shattering. In my eyes, he was becoming the devil himself. His look spoke silently to me saying, "I've got you now." I remembered his rejection of our wedding plans and his fateful fall down the front steps in what turned out to have been a drunken stupor. That same grin echoed silently over and over within me, "I've got you now."

I excused myself and ran to the men's room. My world had been knocked dizzily upside down and inside out. Fear inhabited my body from my scalp to my toes. The clams churned in my stomach. I wanted to throw up but I couldn't. He's out to get me, I told myself. The son of a bitch is trying to kill me! I was convinced that he had poisoned my clam roll. And, his grin meant for sure that he knew his grisly plan was already at work in my stomach and I was helpless to do anything about it. Of all that, at that time, I was dead certain. It took a great deal of time for me to come to understand and accept that I had experienced a severe psychotic break.

It was midmorning, a warm spring Saturday. The backdoor off the kitchen was wide open. Through the screen I could see a sturdily built, bald headed man a little older than me, body arched backward slightly, standing on the brick landing inside the garage. I pushed the screen door out a bit and said "Hello."

"Hello, my name is Ernest Lemieux. I am the new Pastor at the Methodist Church." He smiled and added, "I was curious as to how an Italian like Palanza was on the membership list of the Methodist Church."

How can a Frenchman be a Protestant minister, I thought to myself, unsure of what to make of him, although his friendly demeanor reassured me. "Come in" I said, wondering if he were reading my face, or my mind, since I hadn't been in the church since Jeannie, our first born had been baptized.

We talked for a long time and I sensed from him genuine warmth, a true appreciation of who he had become thus far in life. I felt at home with him. He then spoke at length on how and why he had chosen Eastern Nazarene College as the place to embark on his road to the ministry.

As he rose to leave he smiled, faced Dori and said, "Why don't you both come to church tomorrow."

I was moved by his sermon. I listened and absorbed every word. While the gist of it remains deeply imbedded in my psyche, the text long since has eluded me. However, I have never forgotten the phrase, "And they will beat their swords into plowshares, and their spears into pruning hooks." Those words, unconscious seeds that lay dormant within me for many years, have been resurrected from the depths of my subconscious mind. And, in retrospect they now speak to what was then my blind side insofar as I was unable, at that time, to see them in the light of wisdom. Historically, I had been self-mandated to wield my sword out of fear. The sword and its use as a symbol of my defense against a hostile world would be supplanted with a tool for peace and love; it was to become a plowshare.

I returned the following Sunday and he said, "Rich, I thought you might like to take the collection plate up the left center aisle today."

That was the beginning, like putting my toe in to test the water. I attended Sunday services regularly. I volunteered to serve on the local missionary committee, phoning and calling on prospective newcomers to the church. And, upon occasion, along with other younger members, read passages from Scripture as part of the Sunday Service. Dori and I participated in many of the newly instituted social activities such as picnics and softball. I made and donated masonry repairs to the Parsonage and I coached the church youth basketball team.

We became like father and son on a fishing trip. He baited the hook; I cast my line wherever I wished. And with each cast I sought answers to unfathomable questions. I read six or seven of his philosophy and theology books, whetting my appetite for more. We talked for hours on end about the question of evil, good works verses faith, the crucifixion and salvation, the historicity of Jesus, free will verses determination and suffering and sin.

Ultimately, I became motivated to return to college. He was delighted. He wanted me to become a minister and for a long while I thought about it. I thought about how I loved to smoke, drink, curse and make love with my wife. I thought little or nothing about using others to my own advantage. If anyone were to have told me I was asleep, an unconscious mechanically motivated being, I would have laughed arrogantly in his or her face. At bottom it was ignorance and pride that led me away from that inner invitation, ignorance of what I really was; pride, in that I was determined not to be a hypocrite.

"I am twenty seven years old, married, and I have a two year old daughter. I employ a three-man crew in my masonry contracting business. How in the world could I ever go to Union Theological College?"

"Well," he said, "I don't know, but where there's a will there's a way."

"What's the matter with Eastern Nazarene College. It's close enough for me to commute and I can still support my family. You went there and you came out okay."

"Indeed, why not!"

So it was that I took the plunge. I was not the type to be a minister. I was not worthy enough. It would be hypocritical. Rejecting the call, I entered college and began to make the transition from mason to teacher.

Dori was unsure but, once committed, she never wavered. She stood by me. She handled the household, aided me in my business, and typed all my papers. She gave birth to our second daughter whom we named Dori-Ann. She even agreed to sell our home and live in an apartment while I earned an AB in history with a double minor in philosophy and literature at Eastern Nazarene College, and later an A.M. in History from Boston University. I don't see how I ever could have understood the hardship I caused her. She sacrificed so much and so silently, all with her stiff English upper lip.

To a stranger's eye, Eppy's shop would seem chaotic. Outside four or five old junk cars waited to be stripped. Inside, the walls were decorated over time with used parts from cars long since forgotten. Tools were everywhere, leaning against partially opened drawers, others scattered haphazardly on top of the long workbench and some piled up on one another as though discarded. A square metal pan filled with gasoline and several auto parts tossed into it for soaking waited to be flushed. A new Ford Mustang, front end raised with chains, was hanging from the collar ties, its engine sitting on the concrete floor. An Oldsmobile next to it waited for an oil change. The little room reeked of grease and oil.

"What are you doing?"

Eppy looked up at me smiling from under the hood of the Olds. "What does it look like I'm doing?"

"I don't know, a tune up maybe?"

He straightened his short hunched back upward as much as possible staring and smiled, "See, you're always asking dumb questions."

I first met Eppy when I was in grade school. His three boys were the same age as my two older brothers and me. We played football and baseball in the field diagonally across from their house on Walnut Street. On occasion we played other teams across town; we called ourselves "the Walnut Street Bone Crushers." During the winter we skied on the hills beyond Atwood's Field behind our house and played ice hockey in the swamp off Chauncey Street. I gradually grew closer and closer to Eppy maybe because I had lost my own father. He always treated me like his own son.

I remember the time I had just signed an agreement and put a down payment on a used car. "The damn thing pulls to the right!" Dori said.

"It felt okay to me. And It looks great and it's only a year old," I replied.

"Well, I think we should take it up to Eppy and see what he says."

It was a warm afternoon. Eppy was standing in his driveway. Dori pulled up beside him, rolled the window down and asked, "Can you take this for a ride and tell us what you think?"

"Where'd you get that?"

"From Johnny's Used Cars," I said.

He drove down Chauncey Street, turned right onto Central and right back to his garage. He turned off the ignition, got out, stood several feet away behind the car leaned forward slightly and squinted down one side of the car then moved over and squinted again. After a few seconds he broke the silence.

"Been in a wreck."

"How can you tell?" I asked.

"See here," he said as he ran his hand down the right front fender.

"I don't see anything."

"It pulls to the right," Dori said.

"Yup, it does, it pulls to the right." Eppy agreed.

"I don't see anything," I said

"What the hell's the matter with you," he bellowed, "You blind or something?"

"Has it been in a wreck," Dori asked.

"I think so," Eppy responded.

"What should I do? I signed an agreement and gave him a deposit."

"Give it back to him; tell him you want your money back. All he's got is junk, mostly wrecks that he gets fixed," and then with a smile added, "and sells to chumps like you."

When I told Johnny I had seen Eppy and what he said, I had no trouble getting my money back. He always took care of me like a father should even when I didn't ask him.

Another time after I had left my truck for an oil change I returned to see that Eppy had fit, cut, and cemented a new green carpet. It fit like a glove.

"Looks great Eppy," I said surprised, "Why did you do that?"

"Looked like you needed one; Besides, I had a little time."

"How did you do it?"

"I cut it, and fitted it and glued it. How the hell do you think I did it?"

"Well it sure looks great. How much do I owe you?"

"Oh . . . four bucks."

"Four bucks, Eppy, you're crazy; how could you do that for four bucks?"

"I had the carpet and glue left over."

I handed him ten dollars. He dug into his pocket to make change. "No, no, Eppy ten dollars isn't half enough." Then, mimicking him I chided, "You have to charge more for your work, you damn fool."

He shook his head silently and said, "Thank you."

"Oh no, thank you Eppy. Thank you very much."

Shortly after our wedding Dori and I had bought a used Ford sedan. It was a huge transition upward from the old lemon I got from my brother Willie a year or so earlier. We hadn't had the new car very long before my younger brother Danny asked if he could borrow it to take his girlfriend to the prom. The next morning I got a phone call from Danny telling me that he had had an accident and that the car suffered some damage underneath. I had the car towed to Eppy's for a meeting with the insurance adjuster.

After some time surveying the vehicle the adjuster turned to me and said, "Well, you ought to be able to straighten the frame for a reasonable amount of money."

"I don't think so," Eppy interrupted.

"Why not, that's what we pay for the job all the time?"

"Bullshit! I'm telling you that there ain't no fixin' this frame!"

"What do you mean," he said appealing to Dori and me, "I have it done all the time. I can direct you to someone who will do it for that."

Just then our insurance agent arrived and I told him that the adjuster thinks the frame of my car can be fixed but Eppy said no.

"Why, Eppy?"

"I say you can never straighten out this frame so as the car will ride right. It will always be outta line."

"Then it's totaled," the agent said as he turned to face the adjuster, "Eppy says so."

After they had gone, I thanked Eppy for speaking up for me. "It's only right . . . it's only fair," he said with a warm smile.

Eppy, it seems, was the last of a dying breed from all fields of craftsmanship. The art of repair rapidly declined as new technologies introduced simplified methods and procedures for new installations, repairs no longer were practical. The new technology simply called the diagnosis to determine what had to be replaced. While the philosophical marketing theory of conspicuous consumption has proved to be successful beyond anyone's imagination, the unmentioned downside is the direct inverse increase of waste. Don't fix anything anymore; replace the whole damn thing!

The last time I visited with Eppy he told me that he wasn't feeling well.

"What's the matter," I asked, not overly concerned.

"Oh . . . I dunno . . . Just feelin' lousy, cold in my chest, like maybe bronchitis or something, I guess."

"Seen the doctor?"

"Doctor . . . no, no doctor . . . no need."

"Well, if you are sick you should see a doctor."

I was deeply saddened when Eppy died. In many ways he was the father I longed for but no longer had. He taught me the value of leading a simple, honest and practical life. He was one of the wisest and loving men I have ever known.

True wealth is having infinite capacity to fulfill one's needs and wants without regard to one's income. To some this may seem like a foolish statement yet it is true. Wealth is not measured in money. Happiness in what may appear to be poverty seems miraculous. Maybe! Yet anyone having accomplished it knows the rules governing such a miracle are simple enough to understand though extremely difficult follow.

The first rule is to know the difference between what I am told I need as opposed to what I know I need. And, knowing the difference between what I am told I want verses what I know I want. Although these understandings appear simple they are not as easily attainable as they may seem. One must begin with a correct assessment of one's self, which requires an on-going, penetrating examination of exactly what one expects to get from life. Without this self-understanding one is constantly in danger of being seduced and controlled by the endless societal propaganda asserting that the road to happiness requires material wealth.

The second rule is to truly know one's values. What constitutes value? Scarcity. Look around. There is only one of me; there is only one of you. Only individuals are of infinite intrinsic worth. Everything else, all commodities are instrumental to the individual person. Material possessions are commodities. They are instrumental. I have them; they do not have me. They have no intrinsic value.

I learned this in a rather strange way. Many years ago my father-in-law, while discussing his awareness of the difference between my income as a mason and his as a toolmaker suggested with a bit of pride, "Ye know Richy, if ye put bye fifty cents a week, at the end of the year ye will have saved twenty-five dollars!" He carried no debt. He paid cash for everything from a pair of socks to a new suit.

For several days I chuckled silently in my mind regarding the meager sum he viewed to be a great saving. Then suddenly it struck a chord within me. I found and took away more than a bit of wisdom from his simplistic earthy economic philosophy. Live within your income; carry no debt, maintain your own home; be your own boss physically and psychologically. Learn to live within your means and you can experience happiness. Being happy is a feeling of well being which accompanies the conscious determination to walk successfully in one's own light. This chosen life alone yields true wealth!

Chapter Five

Books

Education is liberation from social indoctrination; how it inspired me and ultimately how it relates to my life's journey and my discovery of who I am was important for me to understand. I was particularly struck by Plato's well-known Allegory of the Cave. It took a long time for me to the gain full appreciation of its true meaning. It required great effort to transition myself from what I thought Plato said to what he wanted me to understand, the difference between knowing and being. Knowledge is necessary, but existential awareness comes only as a result of a change in one's being. For me, that transition was yet to come. In that journey I found allies in the many minds with whom I would commune through books.

Zen and The Art of Archery, was the first book I read on Zen Buddhism. I found it fascinating, chiefly because as an artisan and an athlete I was able to understand the author's advice to relax and detach. For the archer this meant the bow, the arrow and the target need to become as one entity. When such discipline is achieved, the archer, the bow and arrow become one with the target. No longer is the target over there while the archer stands here. The arrow becomes an extension of the bow, the bow becomes one with the archer, and the archer becomes one with the bull's eye! As an athlete it seemed as though I never failed to complete a forward pass when I attained, without thinking, that state of oneness with the ball and the receiver. I experienced similar success when bricklaying, plastering, applying stucco, and cement finishing.

I recall a time when I was building a brick corner. The corner built itself up three feet before I checked its level in both directions or looked to see if it were plumb on both sides and yet they were perfect. I suspect that for any skilled mason, such experiences would be common.

Yet, this book offered me more than a validation of what I had already known to be true from my years as an athlete and a mason. I was fascinated by it and intrigued by a note I found hidden within its pages, an invitation complete with the address, date and times of weekly meetings of a study group in the Boston area on the Sufi teachings by a man named Gurdjieff. I felt a persistent, constant, nagging tug, urging me to dig more deeply into the nature of eastern thought and decided to go. I spent the next few months immersed in the study of Gurdjieff's mystical philosophical works along with several other noted and very worthwhile scholars such as P. D. Ouspensky and Maurice Nicoll who were much more lucid in interpreting the master's thoughts.

What I learned and took away with me was an understanding of the meaning of being sound asleep and that I had to awaken in life, to become conscious of the hypnotic hold that conditioning socialization had on me, to understand that without awakening, one is powerless. Those who are awake and conscious can control their lives while those who are asleep are unconscious cannot. Those that cannot, remain self-victimized, harboring and responding to their countless numberless little personal wants and desires that flood the sleeping mind. Those who have sought and attained will power are awakened in life and are free to choose whatever they wish. They are free from the prison of socialization and their desires and hopes are no longer captive to external authority.

One other and most profound teaching I learned was the difference between necessary and unnecessary suffering. Unnecessary suffering is once again the result of being sound asleep and being victimized by unlimited desires. Those who do not or cannot awaken have no will and must suffer unnecessarily. No one need suffer unnecessarily. On the other hand everyone must suffer necessarily. Everyone must understand and feel another's pain, know that the other needs understanding as well as respect, compassion, and love. For the awakened person it becomes a volitional habit which further liberates the soul from unnecessary suffering.

I decided to browse a used bookstore. I shuffled up and down between the aisles slowly, stopping briefly now and again as a title drew my attention. After a time, toting an armful of books, an orange paperback caught my eye. For reasons of which I was then completely unaware, I was instantly drawn to it. The title read *Mastery Through Accomplishment*. It was written by Hazrat Inayat Khan. I set all the other books down atop the nearest table and turned to the inside cover. The condition of the pages suggested that the book had never been read. The inscription told me that the book had been a gift to someone with an Islamic name. Once again the lure of Eastern mysticism compelled me to want to read this book.

In *Mastery Through Accomplishment*, the teachings of Hazrat Inayat Khan focus with exquisite clarity and contemporary relevance on how our essential spiritual nature can be realized in the material world. For most people, the desire for happiness can only be fulfilled in the realm of everyday life. In fact, the experiences of everyday life provide the substratum, which is essential to the growth of the soul.

I read the book nonstop. I felt as if I was attending a wonderful concert. Truths expressed through a soft, gentle and melodious loving voice resonated inside my whole body as I read. So moved was I that I took advantage of the invitation on the back cover to learn more about The Sufi Order of the West.

The Sufi Order is more tolerant, compassionate, and has a far greater immersion into love than was the Gurdjieff group. I remain, some thirty years later, an aspiring Sufi. I strive to be a lover of wisdom, a ray of God, a messenger of good will, a compassionate soul, a lover of humanity and a genuine pilgrim on the path to enlightenment.

The Way of a Pilgrim, was written by an unknown nineteenth-century Russian peasant and tells of his constant wrestling with the problem of how to pray without ceasing. The challenge is to remember to remain ceaseless in prayer until it continues without effort and ensures that one remains awake. The prayer is powerful yet simple. It reads, "Lord Jesus Christ have mercy on me."

For a while it felt awkward, repeating the simple phrase, "Lord Jesus Christ have mercy on me," over and over, all day, every waking moment. At first it seemed like mumbling to myself, but in time, I was able to recite the prayer internally, in my mind, ceaselessly. I was quite proud of myself and it provided impetus for me to continue on for a number of years. When I felt mastery over it I became aware of change taking place within me. I was better able to remember to remember as time elapsed and I indeed knew that being awake was unearthing a self-awareness of who I am and an increased ability to improve my relationships and strengthen my devotion to the Sufi teachings. Over the years I have, now and then, returned to the prayer in time of need. I find it to have served me unfailingly. It may seem incongruous to some that one would recite a Christian prayer as part of a Sufi practice, but for a Sufi there is no distinction.

Mystics say that if you take a drop of water from the ocean, that drop contains all that is in the ocean; and, all that is in the ocean is contained in the drop. Yet, the drop, apart from the ocean, has no true existence within the context of the reality of the whole since any understanding of the drop as a complete entity is misguided and self-deceptive.

I am on the treadmill. Walking slowly at first and increasing gradually, hands wrapped tightly on the guardrail, my heartbeat moves upward slowly and steadily to 133. I decide to meditate the unity of Judaism, Christianity, and Islam and I become aware once again of the evolutionary oneness of those three religions, their individual uniqueness sustained only by the refusal to see the oneness. Each individual person is like the drop of water apart from the ocean, alienated from the oneness of God and the Universe. My mind wanders further, to the Sufi practice of Ya Ahad, that place of absolute stillness, that place where God resides before vibration or sound, that place of absolute serenity.

Yet another Sufi teaching breaches my reverie. All souls, each of us, are as Rays of God and our individual light is meaningful only when seen within the brilliance of God. We are, each and all, aspects of the Holy Spirit insofar as we are aspects of God. We cannot see the whole any more than our fingers can see our whole body. But we can know the whole just as the fingers know what the body expects of them. Our yearning is unfulfilled yet we have faith and believe that what we yearn for exists, it is the knowing that it does, and that knowing can be found in meditation. So we hope that our beliefs are true, and if we have faith, it is because we know that our beliefs are indeed true. But each of us can only say this for ourselves. Yet, that's enough! If others are able to see their truths and I theirs, our faith is shared and our collective light is increased twofold. We become doubly blest. But if I hide my light, I seal away not only my self from hope, I also weaken my beliefs and have little, if any, faith and can never share my light with the light of others.

Still on the treadmill, I glance at the heart monitor and look again to confirm that my pulse rate is 61, calm, despite the rapid pace of my workout! Continuing on in a meditative state causes me mentally to review the practice of meditation itself. I begin with concentration, the first of the three stages of meditation. I concentrate upon any object, place, or person, any thing I wish. My mind drifts to see, visualize and focus. I see an impatient parent out of control, trying to gain control over a rambunctious child, to the point where the parent becomes the problem. The parent has lost his battle with opposites within, he has hidden his light and is not able to see reality. He is unable to prevent his projections of anger and resentment onto the child and acts upon those feelings by verbally abusing the child. Unconsciously smothering his light, he is unable to tender understanding and love toward the child. He is now overcome with rage, hatred, and resentment, causing much the same reaction in the child. It is the child who suffers the wound inflicted by the parent who more than likely suffered in the same way.

Again my eye catches sight of the heart monitor. Still it reads 61! I focus my thoughts on the abusive parent; I concentrate on that abuse, fully aware that the misplaced anger was the result of the parental inner polar swing. And I also focus on the feelings of the wounded child until I am fully aware and realize that the scar will be carried by the child as had the parent's throughout an entire lifetime. I concentrate on these images until they become a part of me before moving on to the second stage of meditation, contemplation.

I reach for the contemplative state by asking myself what it is like to be that abused child, to suffer the wound inflicted by the parent. It is when I become that child that I have achieved the state of contemplation. Then, I immediately feel the anger, resentment, and rage of both the parent and the child. I see the wounds my own parents inflicted upon me and I know that the only healing possible is the faith they may find in the Crucifixion. Like the abused child who is symbolically nailed to the cross by abusive parents, the parents themselves drive spikes through their own hearts and suffer self crucifixion even more unbearably. And I come to that place of knowing in my meditation and the relief of being able to walk in the light, in the center of my polar opposites, my cross is more bearable and I too am also able to say, "Forgive them Lord, for they know not what they do." Once more, without breaking the rhythm of my trek I glance at the heart monitor and again I see that it remains fixed at 61! I close my eyes and continue.

The third stage is meditation itself. I begin by feeling the power of the universe. As I breathe in the hurt from the wounded child, the parent, and the parental wounded child within that parent, within me and my own parents, I exhale the love, forgiveness, and understanding of that power in the universe of which I am a ray and I shine my light as brightly as possible to reconcile the opposites of suffering and joy, which are inherited by all. I have reached the meditative state, that place where we are offered a momentary glimpse, a holy look and are able to say with our Maker, "I am that I am" and I accept others as they are by turning my light on as bright as possible, my light of detachment, compassion, understanding, my light of love, Divine Love which sustains me. From God's mind, from God's consciousness we become, and to God's consciousness we return. I glance once more at the heart meter and see that my pulse rate remains yet at 61.

She strode down the aisle as if she were wearing the grace of elegance. She was one of the most stunning women I had ever seen in my life. Tall, slim with shoulder length golden hair framing her face. Her bright blue eyes emitted as much as they absorbed while her smile suggested a cautious welcome. As I passed her I felt her warmth inside me.

It was the Columbus Day weekend 1987. I had volunteered to serve on a Sufi Order committee to plan, organize and implement a three-day seminar. During one of the lectures I heard the speaker state, and restate the notion that if you failed psychologically to resolve successfully the first three years of your life you would never reach Nirvana. His words echoed over and over in my mind; that was all I heard, remembered and took away with me.

That evening a dance had been planned for those who wished to relax and socialize a bit before departing. I looked up from the dance floor and by coincidence I saw her again, looking down at what must have been the whole scene, but it was as though she was focusing directly upon me. It was as if her eyes were inside of my eyes. I took frequent peeks up at her as I continued dancing but I was driven to talk to her; I excused myself and tried to find her.

I walked up the right side of the lecture hall past the seat where she had been sitting, but she was gone. My thoughts streamed. I don't know anything at all about her . . . except . . . she is genuine . . . that I do know . . . and it's all I need or want to know. But why am I driven this way . . . what is this strangest of feelings . . . of feeling sadness and joy flood over me . . . as if it's saving me from drowning? I wonder . . . will I ever see her again?

Eighteen months earlier in April 1986 I had undertaken a silent retreat with my Sufi guide, at the Boston Sufi Center in Jamaica Plain. I arrived early enough that Friday afternoon to get settled in one of the small retreat rooms. It was during the second day of the retreat that my guide gave me the practice that I remember best and shall never forget, although, at the time, I was not as fully aware of its impact upon me.

"You are a castle," he said, "You are to carry a torch from room to room in your castle. You are to bring light to every darkened room. You must open each door, shine your light all around the room then close each door behind you and go on to the next room until you have brought your light to every room. You will meet many strange beings in these rooms. They will be afraid of you and you must befriend them. They are hurt. They need your help, they need your light."

A few months after the Sufi seminar I attended a three day healing retreat at the Sufi center on Mount Lebanon in New York and suddenly there she was.

I sat beside her on one of the many picnic benches under the pavilion. I turned my body toward her and with the palms of my hands gently pressed together just below and close to my chest, I bowed my head, and in the formal Sufi manner said, "How do you do? My name is Rachman, my given name is Richard."

"Hello Rachman, I am very pleased to meet you." She responded, "My name is Claire."

My delight drew instantly from her a warm and welcoming smile. "I am so pleased to see you. I hoped we would meet again."

"What does Rachman mean?"

"Compassion, it is one of the names of God."

We talked. She told me that she was a clinical psychologist with a private practice in New York and that she had nearly completed her training to become a Jungian Analyst. I shared with her that I was a high school teacher of history and government and that my interests had urged me to immerse myself in Eastern philosophy and mysticism.

Nature was kind to us those three retreat days. The temperature rose to mid 70's and I saw her from time to time. When it was over, she gave me her business card and I gave her the same information about me. I packed my bags into the trunk of my car and was about to drive off when I saw her standing under a large elm tree on the front lawn of the main house. I walked over to see her one more time. She handed me a four-leafed clover, which she had found along the dirt road. "I wish you good luck on your path, Rachman."

"Thank you for the lucky clover," I replied, "I'll take good care of it."

I drove off waving to her and looking into the rear view mirror to hold as much of her in my sight for as long as possible. It was a long drive back and all the while her image stayed fixed in my mind.

For several days I thought deeply and sincerely about the strange, contradictory feelings swimming around in my head and I couldn't figure out how to resolve them. Finally I called her.

"Claire, this is Rachman."

"Hello, Rachman. It's good to hear from you. How are you?"

"I have for a long while wanted to undertake an analysis, but I haven't found anyone that I might engage with and I was wondering if you might be willing."

She asked me what I knew about Freud and Jung. Did I realize the similarities and the differences? I answered as best I could and in retrospect I must say that I knew more about them than I realized. She was obviously pleased and said we could give it a try. That was the beginning of a five-year exploration into the personal and collective unconscious both for me and for her.

Nearly four years went by before I finally came to know and understand what truly happened. I had met and was influenced by three Guides: The first, who on the second day of my silent retreat with him, suggested through his unconscious to my unconscious that I undertake an analysis. Later, during the Sufi seminar, when I heard the speaker talk directly to my unconscious, telling me that if I didn't do what my first guide suggested I would never reach Nirvana. And it was also there that I met my third guide, Claire. And, although she at first unconsciously eluded me and then nearly got away from me a second time, it was finally through my unconscious that my destiny was realized when she agreed to be my analyst.

How does anyone avoid the self-inflicted deterministic consequences restricting personal freedom that are inherent in our collective value system? I wanted to know how I could overcome and rise above being victimized by the wool over my own eyes. As I saw it, the collective values, which I internalized, had created a society that not only discriminated against Blacks and women, but also promoted a lifestyle of confused worthlessness. I needed to understand where on the path I was if I were to solve these problems and that I should never confuse advancement in life with the advancement of the spirit. That would be a deadly game.

I ask myself, am I strong enough to take on the pain of others. I must try, but pride is the strongest of the deadly sins. I was sound asleep, drunk on my own wine; I was driven, pushed and pulled along by my uncontrolled passion like an emotional sot, unable to control that passion. Such a state of being, at times, and at bottom, was the impetus for my insensitive, cruel and contradictory behavior toward my wife and children.

I remembered and connected once again with a Sufi teaching about a runaway horse and wagon, the driver dragged along behind and desperately trying to keep up. The symbolism is clear. Rather than being pulled and dragged by emotion, it is man's responsibility to climb upon the seat of the intellect, pick up the reins and take control of the runaway emotion. Ultimately, it was with that conviction that I decided to undertake a Jungian analysis.

I found the book *Marriage Dead or Alive* by Adolph Guggenbuhl-Craig, a Jungian Analyst, very helpful insofar as it seemed to speak directly to the marital issues that suddenly arose between my wife and me. What do we do with and to one another when we wed? Do we help or hinder, liberate or restrict one another? What is the power of choice or of commitment, is it to do or to let be?

Any marriage without strife is dead, yet marriages with conflict are alive. When we fall in love, we each see the repressed side of ourselves in the other. Thus, both partners are consumed by joy within their own narcissistic reflection. It is through the resolution of this conflict, brought about by each misguided set of projections that marriage will flourish. And that flourishing begins with knowing who the other truly is, as opposed to what we assume is true. In this way we both become the benefactors and reach an understanding by taking back our own projections, falsely foisted upon the other.

Jungian analysis is like eating an apple. No matter where one takes the first bite one finds it to be the same as the last. Everything that is in the first is in each and all bites. Everything is united with all. To learn one teaching is to learn all the teachings. When one sees the truth of this, one understands unity.

I learned through my own experiences with my own children and as a result of my analysis, that it is best not to disturb the child while sleeping. That will create fear. Let the child awaken unafraid and the child will better find its own way. I was able, through my dream analysis to heal my own childhood traumas by nursing both my masculine and feminine sides to overcome the father in me of unbridled passion and the mother in me of unbridled emotion. I truly came to understand the meaning of love.

Chapter 6
Waiting and Expectations

Seated and sipping tea in one of the booths of the open area café at the Boston Sports Club outpatient clinic I thought about the idea of waiting. I sat there patiently with the quiet expectation that Dori's arthroscopic surgical procedure would restore her knee and that she would no longer suffer pain. Waiting and expecting are inseparable. Every wait generates a different expectation. Every met expectation promotes a further expectation.

I wait with Dori expecting her to complete the intake process and then we wait together for the anesthesiologist and the surgeon. Later I wait—with the larger, more important expectation, that I will next see her smiling and happy again. But that expectation is more of a hope because it remains uncertain and that uncertainty is the lynchpin of the ultimate wait, the wait for death, which we all must ultimately face with existential angst.

We are so caught up with transitional hopes throughout life, so much so that we seldom see our own approaching death. Failure to consciously connect waiting with expectations and awaiting the ultimate future foreboding results in a denial about life and death. We come to forget about the final outcome despite its constant lingering at the edge of every expectation we have in life. So, we wait and wait again and again. At times it becomes irksome, on occasion it may be thrilling or exciting but ordinarily we simply grin and bear it, and life goes on without a thought of death.

He, 37 years old, half my age, stands at the threshold of maturity while I ride the crest of old age, yet both have cause to ponder the meaning of death.

Jimmy was born and remained legally blind his entire life. To the casual observer who saw him cycling around town, it was difficult to tell he was at all handicapped. Moreover, Jimmy's relentless pursuit for literacy ultimately made it possible for him to discourse at the highest of levels in the arts and sciences. It was just about a year ago that Jimmy was diagnosed with cancer of the esophagus. Despite a variety of treatments, including surgeries, it grew and was finally deemed inoperable.

My mind wandered to several conversations during which he showed me some of his work. He was a gifted writer and I said to him, "I wish I had the courage to write, Jimmy, I have wanted to write a book for as long as I can remember. You should be proud of yourself."

"Oh," Jimmy answered, "I'm sure you could if you put your mind to it. What do you want to write about?"

"Well," I responded, "I have read a lot of books by mystics. One thing I noticed was that almost all of them seemed to have a need to explain how they came to be who they are, if you know what I mean."

"I'm sure you can do it," he said with an encouraging smile.

I knew that Jimmy was dying and at that moment my mind raced back fifteen years to the Dana-Farber where I had taken Dori for consultation about further breast cancer treatment. We were frightened. It was a difficult time for us both. During that visit, we were surrounded by images of innocent children, riding tricycles, playing with toys and games. In my mind I saw Jimmy for the first time, even though I had known him for years. I saw the little boy inside this dying young man.

I sat down for a visit. To my surprise, Jimmy was receptive and open about his illness and his prognosis.

"I don't know if I can take any more chemotherapy. You know the body can stand only so much; it makes you so tired and weak; I feel like I am at that point; I don't know if I can go on."

"What kind of time table did the doctor give you?"

"None, my doctor said there is nothing more that he can do for me; there is no way of telling where in my body the cancer has gone; it's just a question of time."

"Would you like me to read a few pages from my memoir? I wrote about you."

"Yes, that would be nice, Richy."

It was after I began reading that I realized the difficulty I was having with my fear and anxiety in coming to terms with my feelings about Jimmy and his fatal illness. And, as I read on I noticed my voice wavering and I cried silently at first. It was hard for me to tell whether I was crying out of sorrow or out of fear for myself. The room was still and filled with absolute silence for a few moments until I heard Jimmy say with obvious satisfaction, "That's nice, Richy."

I asked him what it was like; how did it feel to have come to the end of the road having been unsuccessfully treated for cancer, unaware that I would myself face this same horror. He struggled for a moment or two searching for an answer, looked up and me and said, "I can't explain it, but there's a story that, if you could read it, you'd know."

I Want To Live! by Thom Jones is a classic depiction of life's polarities, its injustice and agonizing suffering on the one hand, and the offerings of its beauty and joy on the other hand, witnessed through the sadness and remorse of a young woman dying of breast cancer. Fully appreciating, during remission, the true fullness of life, she rises amid life's wonders as never having lived before, to have done and be whatever or whomever she wished. And when the pain becomes so unbearable, she prays for the strength to "turn and run the juices" of medication, to subdue the pain and sink into the abyss of death.

Jimmy was right. Any attempt to describe living feelings reduces life to an abstraction, a thought or a series of ideas. Jimmy, in the midst of adversity, of pain and suffering, frustration and anger, faced with hopelessness and despair, remained steadfast. I pray that I will have the strength to do the same.

For me, the ultimate wait has arrived, psychologically, a painfully slow arrival at that. I learned that my symptoms of shortness of breath and coughing were due to blood clots in my lungs. We thought for a long time that my heart was failing but the symptoms had nothing to do with my heart, which was and remains strong and healthy.

It has been nearly a year since I was rushed to the hospital diagnosed with a large rare type of abdominal tumor, a Leiomyosarcoma. I remain an outpatient in the Dana Farber Treatment Center. The initial goal was to shrink the size of the volleyball sized tumor to something more manageable. That meant chemotherapy. The process has been long and wearing. The tumor, which involves two very small yet vital veins leading to the liver, did not shrink and remains inoperable.

The realistic goal is now to extend my life for as long as possible. So far, I suffer no pain whatsoever as I walk hand in hand with death. The question is always with me. What is death? What does it mean to die? Is there an after life? Can I be certain of that? Am I only a carrier of seeds?

Whatever you have embraced and chased throughout your life points to your answer. For me, it is the cultivation of friends, freedom, and the examined life. Is there such a thing as a soul? Is the soul an aspect of my ego? What I have learned and taken from my Jungian analysis and Sufi understanding of the awakened mystical one has made my comprehension keener than it was when I was totally asleep. These and other questions abound and each of us needs, or at least ought, to consider answering them for ourselves. When is a life complete and fulfilled?

With the grace of God, my life has been good. At eighty-two years of age, staring death in the face with serenity and joy, I take solace in the words of Socrates who said of death: we enter into an everlasting sleep or go on to a far better world. Either way I am happy. I have achieved serenity. My struggle with myself in life, my trip, if you will, has caused me to examine myself, thereby obtaining the wisdom to gain freedom and befriend other pilgrims on the path.

For all the strangers who walked part way with me, they on theirs and I on my own path, I thank them and also upon further reflection, I give thanks for their having been so kind to me all through those years. I was and remain blessed. My whole life has been blessed.

All beings, when cognizant of their relationship with one another, no matter the brevity or duration of their experience, present themselves unknowingly to me with a positive or negative offering that, if I remain aware, I am able to utilize for my own enlightenment. That has been the story of my life. Like electronic particles in the physical world we, as individuals, are all in relationship with each other and with all things. We give and receive unconsciously yet it is all so fleeting. I often wonder how many have helped me without my knowing. I also lament those I have impacted negatively; for that, I am truly sorry.

Yet unavoidable concerns remain that plague and pain me which would or could not have arisen were my death instant. The worst of them is the necessary suffering I must endure seeing those who are most dear to me, my wife, daughters, my grandson, face my demise. It is the most difficult part for me.

Chapter 7

Teaching

Dori screamed as my Fiat sports car bolted forward from the impact. Yet somehow, I remained calm, unnerved. And, I wondered to myself, as if in a meditative state, if we both would be flattened out upon the pavement by the onrushing cars behind us. Reacting to Dori's horrific screams with my left hand on the wheel, I placed my right hand tenderly upon her shoulder. Simultaneously, I thought of my daughters, Jeanne and Dee, of their future welfare without parents and I concluded that they would be okay, even as I continued to comfort my wife. I wondered later how I could have coped with so much chaos so calmly. All the while, for me, time stood still. It had all taken place simultaneously, not one episode after another, but all at once.

I felt the car slowly begin to turn, ultimately 180 degrees while moving obliquely into the furthest right hand lane as we came to a stop without rolling over as I feared we would. I looked up to see what seemed like infinite light showering us with the grace of God. All traffic had stopped. We were safe. We were alive! I was instantly relieved, but Dori remained greatly shaken, still in a state of panic. Thankfully, once sedated, she became calm and we were driven home and tucked ourselves into bed.

The next day felt like a regular school day. Although I cannot recall a single detail, I was conscious in the sense of being present with every class. Finally time seemed to resume again and I felt the trauma to be as an overwhelming, tiresome experience. I slept for several hours.

In the end, I became convinced that time is an illusion, an abstract concept and as such we absorb the idea through social conditioning that time exists and we never question it. Since that accident, for me, everything that ever existed is at once somewhere in the universe of time and we simply pass through events.

For me this experience was another validation of my belief that if I am able to achieve free will, I will see through and become awakened in life and can achieve my destiny. I had, in this episode, a glimpse of eternity, a higher level of being which I desperately wanted to reach. It would be through my years in the classroom that I would finally master that quest.

Once we set our goals in life we are trapped. No longer are we in life but of life and we lose the oneness with the Creator and Sustainer of life, that which in a word may be called peace. By clinging to the objective world we create a dualism in our minds. The problem results from seeing life as an end in itself rather than the means to an end. This I believe is at the root of disharmony within the individual.

We need to understand where we are on the path if we intend to solve the dualistic dilemmas that surface. One should never confuse advancement in material well being with advancement on the spiritual plane. That is a deadly game and it is taking place in all social institutions.

Awakening to life is a slow evolutionary process whereby the painful awareness of habit, customs and indoctrination begin to stir and arouse the question, "Why" leaving one with feelings of disillusionment, of being dismembered from self, and disappointed with society.

I sit reflecting upon the volume of human and economic resources extended on my behalf over the past seven days. Three emergency room visits leading to three hospital stays, inexplicable cost in treasure, family suffering, including my own. Combined efforts from the full cabaret of medical technicians, nurses, doctors in training and specialists, all serving this coordinated effort on behalf of an old man. I reflect further upon this army as a force for good moving forward with banners waving.

I contrast this kind, benevolent human activity to the clear and conscious efforts of the very same nation through wars to manipulate, overpower, destroy, maim, kill and crucify people and I ask, "What's wrong with my head?" And, I cry in wonderment. I cry with amazement and I cry with disgust, hopelessness, and despair. For why do we heal an old man and watch silently while so many babies die?

But, the more fundamental question remains of how to resolve the directly opposing and opposite sides of understanding within all. There is an eternal struggle with the tug of opposites within us. It isn't until we understand and overcome this tendency to sink to the extremes and we are able to find a third way that we can hope to have a glimpse, a taste if you will, of everlasting, eternal bliss, whereby simultaneous suffering and joy supplant the battle between pleasure and pain.

The song of life is played on a kind of distorted harmonica where most of us only know the two notes at either end. They clash in unrelenting cacophony. The beautiful harmony of life can only be heard when one plays all of the notes on a perfectly tuned instrument. This is the function of the third way and the real purpose for education.

During my first classroom position at Quincy Junior College I learned a few things about how different frames of reference impacted my teaching. I had a student who seemed to devour my lectures and discussions as though they were his favorite meal. I expected great things from him. But, when I graded his first Western Civilization exam I saw that it was blank. Not a word was written in response to the questions I had posed. At the end of the next class I asked the student what had happened, why he hadn't answered a single question.

"You didn't ask me anything I know."

"Well what do you know?" I responded, mystified.

"I know a lot about the Byzantine Empire," he said.

I suddenly understood. I asked him if he would write what he knew about the Byzantine Empire. He sat at the desk and filled three bluebooks. His response was excellent.

Much has been said about the student as a unique individual and the value of individualized instruction. Yet, individualized instruction is impossible unless the instructor is able to detach and accept things and people as they are. To see students as a class is to succumb to an illusion.

The idea of a class is very much like any pattern we observe. That is, in actuality, we project it from within ourselves and then convince ourselves that that pattern is truth. Similarly, when numbers of people come together to learn, we come to believe there is something out there which we call a class that fits this predetermined inner formatory pattern which we ourselves have projected. Thus, we create a relationship between students and teacher, which in fact exists only in our own minds.

The mystical teaching I found the most profound yet most difficult to assimilate holds that if you disagree with someone then you do not understand that person. When the listener is able to successfully see the other from the light of that other's frame of reference then his own understanding becomes enhanced, his consciousness is elevated and his previously pious judgmental mind is cast aside. Letting go of one's own vision long enough to see and fully comprehend the vision of others, to see with detachment rather than for the sake of argument, or to grade an exam, is to really see. Letting go, detachment, is the path to enlightenment. I gave him an "A."

Y ears later, while teaching United States History at Mansfield High School, I had a student who earned a "D" for the first quarter, a "C" for the second quarter, a "B" for the third quarter. In the fourth quarter he earned an "A." I gave the student an "A" for the year.

Almost immediately I got a call from the Guidance Department Head requesting my presence.

"Richy", he said, "This student's final grade is not correct."

"Why not, what's wrong with it."

"It doesn't average out right."

"Tests and quarterly grades," I responded, "measure a student's progress. Averaging the results do not measure a student's final achievement. Assessment of where he is at the end of the course is what he has achieved."

"Oh, well, we cannot do that here. We have to average all four term grades together to reach a grade to put on his transcript."

I took the transcript in hand and changed all three of his earlier quarterly grades to "A's" and handed the transcript back.

"Do you really want to do that?"

"Yes," I replied.

"OK," his lips muttered.

J ung's "statistical man" described in his, *The Undiscovered Self* may have significant value with regard to analysis of data and gathering general information. However, commonly accepted procedures which teachers have acquired, while they may be useful, are such only if the teacher realizes that they are not applicable to specific persons. This may be better understood if one sees how it relates to the idea of dualism, that is, energy is expended to make the students conform to what is inside the system, never questioning the system itself.

Once the teacher is able to separate from the idea of the management system, the teacher is then in a position to begin work with individuals and see them as individuals and true teaching then becomes possible.

A good teacher helps to open the student and himself to the relevance of all things to each individual, to others and to all. Nature is the greatest of teachers because she teaches by being; she teaches the handiwork of the Divine, the unity of all, the symbiotic relationship of all with all. The word teacher is misunderstood and misused in contemporary society. It is a product of man's dualistic thinking that has grown out of the rise of science during the Renaissance when authoritarianism promoted the infallibility of scientific authority. The teacher has become the authority in a system that apes the method of science. The student becomes socialized rather than liberated. Jesus' use of parables may well point to the answer to this ethical question. Teaching is a path to individuation, enlightenment, and wholeness of self. The teacher is the student and the student is the teacher.

Unfortunately that is not what exists. Education today embodies the dualistic fallacy that separates the student from himself and convinces him that education is a means to an end rather than an end in itself. Consequently the focus falls on preparation for work as the sole objective rather than preparation for life. The process of real education is on-going and never-ending and as such should result in a personal philosophy of life for each unique and infinitely valuable person.

If absolute truths exist they can never be known by anyone. One must be satisfied with one's own coherent view of life, tempered by the understanding that this view is immutable. Change is the only constant in life and those who embark upon the creation of their own philosophy of life are indeed buffeted by this constant flux. The work is never done.

At present, I ponder a philosophy of life, which embraces all truths, including those of others, which we would rather discard out of hand. Armed with such a deeper and higher degree of understanding, I hope to be able to integrate the truths of others into my own sphere of truth. We are all teachers; we are all students.

I needed a job. A friend of mine scheduled an interview with the Superintendent of Schools in Mansfield. He perused my resume and said, "Oh, too bad, I just hired someone as Principal in one of our elementary schools but I do have a teaching position at the high school if you are interested." I thought about it momentarily and agreed to take the position at the salary step he offered which to me seemed fair. He then suggested and scheduled a meeting for me with the high school principal.

The Principal's reaction, realizing that I was already to be recommended by the Superintendent for School Committee approval, and concerned about some of the questions and thoughts I raised, appeared deeply suspicious of me thinking that I might be a troublemaker. I sensed this and accepted the position reluctantly; I assumed, based upon his reaction, that I would be uncomfortable at Mansfield High School, but I needed the job and I hoped it would afford me the time to find a principalship in another school district.

My observations proved to be correct. But the Social Studies Department Head, Tony, who did not have the opportunity to interview me, I sensed correctly early on, would be vastly different. Administrator, supervisor, teacher, mentor, colleague, and friend, he proved to be superb. Never before or since have I been more correct in my intuition. I remained teaching at Mansfield High School until I retired twenty-two years later. During the last forty years our respect and friendship has steadily grown.

It was surprising to me that I stayed for so long in Mansfield. I never believed I would. I've thought about this many times and can attribute it to my relationship within the Social Studies Department and the seriousness of our work. The expectations were clear and I felt like I was making a real contribution. For the first time, I began to feel that I was a real teacher. I learned more and more about social studies curriculum and how it related to my effectiveness in the classroom and my relationship with my students. I was truly happy there even though my experience in Mansfield also caused me much anguish and heartache.

The contrast between my daily classroom and departmental experience and my relationship with the principal could not have been starker. We disagreed it seemed about almost everything that was important and we conflicted constantly about what a real education was. I didn't realize until recently how important this man, who seemed so out of touch, almost as evil, was to my own enlightenment. I had always been content to see him as an enemy who had to be defeated and I reveled in the fact that in all of our disputes he never succeeded. I didn't realize how he drove me to confront my own inadequacies.

There are so many examples and instances, too numerous to recount, but one stands out as representative of how far apart we seemed to be. The principal always viewed me as a maverick out of step with the goals of the institution. He believed that my teaching was somehow subversive and detrimental to the school. He expected me to skew my classes in such a way as to undermine his and indeed all authority and promote anarchy in the same way that he viewed the efforts of my department head and colleagues to change the culture of the school.

In his attempts to uncover my subversive activities he insisted on evaluating my class when studying the Constitution and the police powers. I saw this as a mildly veiled attempt to set me up to fulfill his expectations about me. I was convinced that his motives were dishonorable and I justified in my efforts to thwart them. I danced artfully around the issue and shared a hearty laugh about it later in the department office. I didn't realize it at that moment, but it was becoming a game, a game that I was determined to win.

For the next several years I was consumed with this struggle, as I know he was. Yet I was strangely happy. I felt myself to be part of a genuine effort to create a better school and I saw the principal as the roadblock. Everything was black and white for me, neatly defined and I was sure that I was right. I worked tirelessly and ultimately successfully for his removal. I saw this as a triumph but not until much later did I realize that the real triumph was my own awakening.

I was my own "helper;" I had become accustomed to working alone—"moonlighting"—a few Saturdays during the school year and I enjoyed it. It provided a change of pace from classroom teaching. Working alone, I became efficient. I knew just what I needed, when I needed it and how I wanted it. I always knew where to find my tools and I didn't give myself any sass.

It was a beautiful Saturday morning when I tossed my small mortar box, mason's hoe, my hock and trowel, pointing trowels, both wooden and rubber floats, and several buckets to carry water and mortar into my old battered truck. I picked up mortar cement, some clean screened brick sand, and then grabbed a coffee "to go".

As I drove to the job site, I thought about Plato's remark that a son should follow in his father's footsteps; that the son of a doctor become a doctor. I had struggled mightily to escape that, remaining a mason for the rest of my life, being one of them. Yet, I think I am now, at this moment, able to understand what he may have meant, though, still, I can't accept it.

I mused further on the thoughts of Karl Marx, that the rise of technology and mass production had alienated the worker from a sense of purposeful being. That the laborer's work, limiting him to a mere part of the whole job, denied him any sense of accomplishment, of creating and seeing, from beginning to end, the whole product of his labor. But, that wasn't true I thought, not for me, not for the artisan. The tools of the trade, the hawk and trowel, haven't changed much in centuries. To approach a job, such as this one, with an agreed contractual plan to follow, performing every task to completion yields a satisfaction beyond belief.

As I begin to apply the stucco on the foundation wall, I find myself in harmony with the weather and the material. Like an automobile radiator cools its engine, the radiator of the universe, the temperature, sunlight, and the gentle breeze cools me, as well as the concrete. My tools become an extension of my hands. I feel the evenness of flow beneath my trowel as I run the mortar up from below the loam line.

I sense I am at one with the job, with myself. I am happy, concentrating on spreading the stucco, transforming and almost becoming the wall while meditating on the creative power of the universe and the simple beauty of the work. I am at once both the recipient and the servant of the universe; I feel important, of value; I am the link between the stuff and the creative hand of nature. At this moment I see and know the meaningfulness of my being. For the first time, I feel fortunate to have learned and acquired my father's skills.

N o one has lived life more alienated than I have and at the same time, few have come to experience as I have the liberating and rich fullness of everyday existence. Yet, even those who experience such richness of fulfillment ever free themselves to partake of the poetry of life by reconnecting on a conscious path and experiencing the real material state in the universe, while simultaneously knowing their abstract place in society. Life is poetry; we are all poets. Poetry heals the wounds of alienation by the poet's experiences of wholeness, by becoming simultaneously attuned with self and the universe. Putting on stucco, like writing poetry, reunites the self as it dissolves the prison of alienation.

Once again I think to myself, I make my own music and follow my own melody; I do not tire for I do not labor; my work is my art and my art is my sustainer. I am the creative force, on this job, at this wall in this moment in time, doing and being who I am. The work becomes an aspect of my very existence and I enjoy that state of serenity and, as a result, the quality of my art nears absolute perfection.

I t was about 2 PM when "I floated off" the last section of stucco and I stretched upward to shake the knots out of my legs. It was then that I saw a huge boulder only a short distance away at the edge of the wood. It had a smooth rather strange slope, giving the appearance of being heavier at the bottom than the top and for some reason it caught my eye. Then I thought I saw slight movement in the leaves resting alongside its base. I took the garden hose, still running, and placed my thumb over the opening, forcing a stream of water hard against the flat side of the boulder, just for the fun of it. As I watched the water splash and then trickle down onto the leaves, again something moved. I looked closely and I found a brown toad, almost indistinguishable from the coloring of the leaves it rested among. I laughed aloud as I stooped to peer into his little world and said, "Oh! Excuse me, Mr. Toad. I didn't mean to frighten you and I didn't mean to get you wet."

The toad's eyes bulged from the sides of his head and his nose pointed directly up at me, his bottom now bolstered against the base of the boulder and I thought I heard him say, "Oh, you didn't, eh."

I leaned down further until I could clearly see the edge of his white belly, mostly buried in and among the leaves. He seemed coiled inside, ready to spring at a moment's notice, like a fighter jet on a runway.

"No, I didn't; I am truly sorry," I said and then asked, "What are you doing here?"

"I am looking for my family."

I knelt down only inches away. He didn't flinch, his nose pointed at my face, eyes bulging laterally, belly floating up and down with his breathing, as was mine. I studied him intently and I wondered what it was like to be a toad, sitting against a boulder in a world that he could never fathom, when suddenly I heard him ask, "My family, where are they?"

"I don't know," I answered. "I haven't seen any other toads today."

Then I looked up into the clear blue sky, overcome with awe at the magnificence of the universe and I immediately understood the toad, whose right eye saw nothing but the grey flatness of the boulder and whose left eye saw only the leaves and I realized that he and I were not so different.

Chapter Eight

Family

My battle with the high school principal was the best thing that ever happened to me, although I didn't realize it at the time. All relationships are good even though they don't seem to be and we learn from all of them, even the unpleasant ones. This all came true again in my relationship with Dori, my wife of nearly 60 years. And that struggle was as bitter and enduring as the other one; it was not resolved until I was able to change myself, but in the end I succeeded.

In a healthy relationship, wisdom, love and harmony reign. There is no last straw. Unity releases the chains of detention, love provides the bond of retention, the two become one. Fighting battles, never surrendering, become the prerequisite to the Royal Marriage. Armed with compassion, understanding, and patience, the goal is resolution, the means a strong desire. Finding the other in each other, discovering yourself in her as she discovers herself in you. These are the answers.

In my dream a tall slender young woman hosted a wedding ball in her cordial palatial home. The ballroom was "sunken" one step down from the main floor. I stood upon the raised section at one end of the room watching as she walked across the ballroom floor toward me, stepped up along side me and asked, "Would you like to dance with me?"

"Nothing would please me more," I replied smiling, noting that she was much taller than I. Guiding her off the platform, lightly into my arms, she returned my smile with a whispered laugh suggesting she also was aware of the differences in our height.

My left hand clasped her right hand and my right arm lay lightly around her back. We danced, as do skilled skaters gliding effortlessly over ice. Our bodies traced lightly enabling each to sense every physical aspect without actually touching.

She seemed happy, as was I. I felt joy beyond belief, ecstasy beyond comprehension. It was an experience to cherish. We talked as if we were the oldest and most intimate of friends. Then, looking into her face I saw she was weeping and I whispered, "It's okay to cry."

"Why?" she asked.

"Those who cry feel and understand more than those who cannot," I said and I kissed her lightly on the cheek. It was then that I noticed we were the only ones on the ballroom floor.

I awoke this morning with a vision of Dori's face and I thought to myself how time has changed both of us. I saw how I have become like her and she has come to mirror me. I see in myself her face as I see myself in the faces of my daughters Jeanne and Dee and in my only grandson, Luke.

I learned long ago that God is everywhere. Since God is all there is and since we are aspects of what is, then God indeed is everywhere. God is all, therefore we are all aspects of God. I have become Godlike by becoming like Dori as she has become like me, as we to our girls and as we to our grandson. I must therefore act in accord with what I innately know to be God's wish. If we are at all conscious and aware we will see God in every person, place or thing and cannot do anything but act according to His will. We see God in the countless faces of others. I stand in awe of His beauty. His silence speaks loudly to my being, His ever presence in All.

I recall my Sufi master, Hazrat Inayat Khan saying, "The qualities of all things are to be found in their spirit rather than in the things themselves." This rang so true to me as I remembered my mother.

As an aspect of our personality each of us has a Trickster. This Trickster has an uncanny knack for getting us to do impulsively something we would not consciously do. Sometimes it leads us to behave in ways for which we are soon sorry. But, quite often, as a result of the Trickster, we find ourselves facing some demon which we normally would not have had the courage to face and we can thereby be transformed; our understanding increases; our fears melt away; our anger dissipates and we become wiser.

On Thursday, March 3, 1994, I learned that my mother had died. I became saddened, bewildered, and quiet. My path had been a struggle to separate from family, especially from her. Over the years, I learned that letting go and detaching was the only way I could be free. I also learned that letting go of my parents and family was the only way that I could allow each of them to also be free. All this I knew. And I thought I had made peace within myself.

And then impulsively I seized the opportunity to speak at her funeral service and to thrust myself back into the center of it again. My brothers and sisters were delighted, but I was told that they expected me to speak for them all! I knew in a flash that the Trickster had gotten to me again. I didn't want to speak for the whole family. I wanted to speak for myself alone. I was trapped. My Trickster was forcing me to confront my dilemma of being myself while speaking for everyone. I didn't say a word, but felt the stifling pressure of a monster that threatened to devour me; but this time it was different although nothing had really changed, except me. I was finally able to be myself and yet reenter the world of selfless family expectations that had always been my experience and to do it without relinquishing my individuality. I was finally able to be myself and also be accepted by them. I had come to see and understand differently and I hoped that they had done the same.

I don't know that I would have ever dared to give that eulogy if my Trickster hadn't forced me to look deeper into my own heart and make me realize that I had finally come to truly and unconditionally love my mother and my family.

I share with you the story of an old woman who lay dying, comforted by her parish priest at her bedside. As she spoke, the priest saw her fear that she had not been devout enough to be received into heaven and that this caused her to tremble with anxiety. Studying her hands, gnarled and worn from a lifetime of selfless service to others, with a soft gentle voice he said, "When you meet Saint Peter at the Gate, just show him your hands."

Life blankets the Soul. To some of us Mother, at times you appeared to be woefully willful, emotionally unbridled and deliberately stubborn in your ways. But circumstance constrains all of us. Imprisoned in time, space, social conditioning and in our own narcissistic projections, we each of us are our own worst enemies. Unlike the game, we cannot throw the cards back and wait for the next hand. Our task is to make the best with what we are given.

At this point I'd like to share a well known poem by John Godfrey Saxe (1816-1887) about six blind men and an elephant. It conveys the thought I have more eloquently than anything I could have written myself.

It was six men of Indostan
To learning much inclined,
Who went to see the Elephant (though all of them were blind),
That each by observation
Might satisfy his mind

The First approached the Elephant,
And happening to fall
Against his broad and sturdy side,
At once began to bawl:
"God bless me! but the Elephant is very like a wall!"

The Second, feeling of the tusk,
Cried, "Ho! What have we here?
So very round and smooth and sharp?
To me 'tis mighty clear
This wonder of an Elephant
Is very like a spear!"

The Third approached the animal,
And happening to take
The squirming trunk within his hands,
Thus boldly up and spake:
"I see," quoth he, "the Elephant
Is very like a snake!

The Fourth reached out an eager hand,
And felt about the knee.
"What most this wondrous beast is like
Is mighty plain," quoth he;
"'Tis clear enough the Elephant is very like a tree!"

The Fifth, who chanced to touch the ear
Said: e"en the blindest man
Can tell what this resembles most;
Deny the fact who can
This marvel of an Elephant
Is very like a fan!"

The Sixth no sooner had begun
About the beast to grope,
Than, seizing on the swinging tail
That fell within his scope,
"I see," quoth he, "the Elephant
Is very like a rope!"

And so these men of Indostan
Disputed loud and long,
Each in his own opinion
Exceeding stiff and strong,
Though each was partly in the right,
And all were in the wrong!

So oft in theologic wars,
The disputants, I ween,
Rail on in utter ignorance
Of what each other mean,
And prate about an Elephant
Not one of them has seen!

Everything has its opposite; for true there is false, for up there is down, for mind there is matter. This dualistic paradigm causes us to perceive opposites as separate entities, while in actuality they are different ends of the same reality, the farthest reaches if you will of a spectrum where each of us touches different parts of the elephant. Each has his or her particular aspect of truth artfully disguised as the whole truth.

In their search for truth, scientists and mystics are also groping, but at opposite ends of the same line; the scientific school is epistemologically based in rationalism and abstract thought; the mystic is epistemologically based in intuition, steeped in feeling. Each sees only part of the elephant.

My personal model of the universe incorporates both the scientific and the religious schools of thought. Metaphysically it posits monism. I believe that mind and matter are one and the same. Theologically this assumes pantheism; the universe itself is One Supreme Being that manifests as both mind, which is the spiritualization of matter and the source of free will, and, simultaneously, as matter, which is the materialization of spirit and the force of determinism.

At one end of this continuum is free will, the creative force of the universe, while at the other end of the continuum are the immutable mechanical laws of the physical universe itself. Everything, including each person, is at once both a free individual and a captive expression of the body universe. Freedom is both real and illusory.

The dualistic paradigm, however, dictates that looking inward is a subjective and suspect act equated with the mystical and religious while looking outward is an objective, honest act equated with science. Moreover, trapped in the dualistic paradigm we fragment ourselves further by assuming intuition as the basis for arriving at truth to be fallacious in nature and reason to be objective and reliable. In so doing, we lose the crucial understanding that by looking inward we can better see out.

Intuition is infinite and eternal and the real window to truth, but it is tied to the imagination and can suffer flights of fantasy. Reason is finite; it is verifiable in time and space. While alone it cannot reveal truth it is the necessary guard against intuitional fantasy; yet without intuitional inspiration reason will grope forever against an unfathomable elephant.

Chapter Nine

Luke

Toward the One, the perfection of Love, Harmony, and Beauty
the Only Being, United with all the Illuminated Souls, who form
the Embodiment of the Master, the Spirit of Guidance.

Sufi Prayer

My grandson Luke served as the ultimate inner teacher for me by opening my eyes to the true meaning of the illusive Sufi Prayer. He taught me that all the people I have written about, as well as all of the others who have entered into my life, including those whom I have misunderstood and mistreated, have served as eyes for me to see more clearly.

We are all given two lives. It is with the first life that we become aware of our social existence, that public being of which we are all aware and know to be the life that stems from working for financial compensation and sustenance within the bounds of societal ethics. The second life is our inner or private life, that secretive life of which each alone is aware, that life of creative thinking, self-reflection, evaluation and criticism.

Few realize however that there is a third life, which is the life you fashion of the other two and that it is the only life that will bring true happiness. This divine creation stems from the sovereign wisdom of the teacher within each of us. While all aspire to this, only those who succeed will find their inner guide, the liberated self that best manages the complex relationship of each to self and to all others.

Awakened one morning from a dream in which I reviewed in an instant the countless relationships I have experienced throughout my life, I saw the need to incorporate those relationships into this manuscript in order to better understand the Sufi prayer. My wish is that all the people whose paths I have crossed in my life, briefly and intermittently or constantly and enduringly might also see, realize and understand the web of human connections to which we are drawn and become unified with the One as clearly as I. To come to know, realize and accept that the You that is Me is the Me that is You. That the One is the All and the All is the One; it is the face of God in my face, in your face, and in all faces. The boundless feeling of my joy, as well as the depth of my sadness are expressions of God.

When I first laid eyes on Luke the day that he was born I saw and felt the light of love and joy of God in his heart and eyes. Little did I realize at that moment how much he would need me to be there for him. At that moment of joy I could not have imagined how many nights he would sleep over with Buppy and Narn in his own room upstairs, how many fears I would allay, how many words of encouragement I would utter, how many bruises I would sooth, yet at the same time how much fun and joy we would share and as he grew so quickly before my eyes, how many baseball and soccer games I would attend and how many talks we would have about so many things that flood the mind of a boy becoming a man.

Why do grandparents like myself dote on their grandchildren if not to provide them the opportunity they themselves never had, that opportunity they see in the infant, youth, teen or young person? Is it for them the chance to create a new Eden of birthrights wealth, that quality set of circumstances at birth that gives rise to the greatest opportunities in life itself? Grandparents, whose candles are near extinguished having spent most of their time on the path, learning by trial and effort and are now able see the gift of opportunity at birth essential to their own faith, try to pass this Eden on to their grandchildren to enable them the best chance for themselves and others in this world. In so doing, we help to execute God's design.

This was what I wanted for my grandson. This was why I never criticized or scolded him in any way. Some would have seen this as indulgence and I heard that criticism many times. It wasn't because I refused to see anything he did as wrong. It was because I wanted to spare him unnecessary suffering. I suffered unnecessarily for a long time and I was resolved not to contribute to this in any way, any longer. I guess this is the point I want to make more than anything. We have a tendency to torture ourselves with unnecessary suffering, suffering that we create for ourselves and in so doing we also foist it on others, those closest to us and those we love most are the convenient and the easiest targets. How different it would be if we could only stop and see what we do.

Unnecessary suffering is exactly the opposite of necessary suffering. It is allowing pain, agony and grief to be put upon oneself, for not being able to detach, let go and assess, at the moment, that which is truly troubling in the situation at hand. I grieved gladly to spare him any needless unnecessary suffering. In so doing I learned to understand life as it really is and that this is the only way to reach the third life and find the pathway back to my own Garden of Eden and to know what real love is. My resolve to practice this in my relationship with Luke brought me to the place where I truly understood the love of God.

Necessary suffering is bearing witness in silence and feeling the pain of those who suffer unnecessarily. Necessary suffering is kept secret along with prayerful thoughts to help those who are injured physically and or psychologically. Necessary suffering brings both pain and joy simultaneously to the person who becomes aware and sorrow for those who suffer pain needlessly and is simultaneously grateful for the understanding of the meaning of true suffering. When nailed to the Cross Christ said, "Forgive them Lord for they know not what they do." Necessary suffering brings pain, the pain of others, "Who know not what they do."

I often think of my wife Dori and my children Jeanne and Dee and feel sad about the times that I was not in control of myself and consequently wounded them psychologically. Unfortunately, until they learn to detach and accept what is as opposed to what in their minds ought to be and are able to absolve their own wounds, they will remain for all time under the negative influence of my hurtful words and deeds. Yet for me, despite the sorrow of my past actions, I remain grateful for having learned and brought that to an end.

The Garden of Eden is everywhere and always. It lies within the power of each person. The return path to the Garden of Eden is liberation, when necessary, to detach oneself from abstract thinking. The capacity for detachment and letting go, and to see, understand and accept totally is the return path. It is as the Sufis say, "To be in the world, but not of it."

The night before my operation at Brigham and Women's Hospital, Luke said, "I love you Buppy and I would not be who I am today if not for you."

In this life Luke you are my grandson. In past lives I suspect you may have been my grandfather, I possibly your son, a brother or a best friend. For me, the knowledge of you feels internal. We have always been connected and will remain connected in ways we have yet to discover.

I love you too,

Buppy